SOCCER

IQ

Things That Smart Players Do

DISCARD

DAN BLANK

Welcome to *Soccer iQ*, the best-selling soccer book on Amazon.

If you would like to place a bulk order for 20 or more copies of this book at a discounted price, please email me at coach@soccerpoet.com.

When you finish this book, I invite you to take the free *Soccer iQ* quiz at www.soccerpoet.com.

I hope you'll be my Twitter friend: @SoccerPoet

For Izzy

TABLE OF CONTENTS

FOREWORD

In early 2009 I was the Head Coach at Ole Miss and had just lost my top assistant. There were a lot of excellent candidates interested in the position. Dan was already on my staff as a volunteer and I had to decide whether or not he should be promoted into the position of lead assistant. At the same time, the head coaching job at Arkansas, another SEC school, had come open. I was speaking to our team captains about promoting our volunteer assistant into the top spot. They didn't really know Dan very well and were skeptical. It was during the course of that discussion that I had my *Aha!* moment. I said to the captains, "Well I can tell you this, I sure as heck don't want him taking the job at Arkansas!" And just like that, Dan became my lead assistant at Ole Miss.

The 2009 season was one of the most enjoyable, memorable and successful in my fifteen-year career at Ole Miss, and Dan was a major contributor to our success. Among his many responsibilities, Dan was in charge of our defense. I gave him complete autonomy to organize our defense any way he saw fit. And just to make his life a little more difficult, I took our All-American center back away from him and converted her into a center midfielder.

We started two freshmen, a sophomore, and a senior across the back that year. Our goalkeeper was a 5'5" sophomore, walk-on – the shortest goalkeeper in the conference. And that season Ole Miss posted the best goals-against average in the SEC.

In April of 2010 I accepted the head coaching job at the University of Georgia and I brought Dan along with me, again leaving him in charge of the defenders. One of the players we inherited on the Georgia roster was Laura Eddy. Eddy was the SEC Freshman of the Year as the Bulldog's central defender. And just like I had done at Ole Miss, I immediately converted our best defender into a midfielder, leaving a gaping hole in the center of our defense. It didn't matter.

In 2010 Georgia posted the best goals-against average in the SEC. I don't think it's a coincidence. In the history of the SEC, no coach had ever led the conference's best defense in consecutive years at different universities until Dan did it. I think Georgia has the best defense in the conference because we have the best-coached defenders in the conference. Make no mistake – my assistant knows his stuff!

This book is fantastic in both its content and simplicity. As I read it, the one thought that kept popping into my head was, *Why has no one done this before? Why has no one put this information down on paper?*

Too many players get to the college level without a sufficient level of fundamental street smarts. That's what this book gives you – street smarts. It's about being a thinker, not just an athlete, and not just a talent. This book gives you pearls, *bite-sized nuggets,* that are easy for your brain to digest. And best of all, you can implement these strategies right away to immediately become a better player.

You've chosen to read what may be the most useful soccer book ever written. Enjoy!

Steve Holeman – Head Coach
UGA Soccer

INTRODUCTION

Did you know that the 1960 presidential election between John F. Kennedy and Richard Nixon was, in large part, decided by some beads of sweat? The two candidates participated in our nation's first nationally televised presidential debate. The stakes couldn't have been any higher. Millions of Americans would tune in to decide who they felt would best lead our country. The winner of that debate would likely win the presidency.

Aware of Nixon's propensity for perspiration, Kennedy's handlers cranked up the thermostat in the television studio for hours before the debate began. When the candidates arrived, the studio was uncomfortably warm and stuffy. The hot studio gave Nixon fits. While Kennedy looked cool and composed and qualified to lead a nation, Nixon's face dripped with sweat, giving the impression that he was rattled and nervous and anything other than presidential. The iconic image of that debate is Nixon using a handkerchief to wipe the beads of sweat from his face.

Kennedy was the runaway winner of that debate and his success carried over into the voting booths. Kennedy became our nation's 35th president and the world's most powerful man. All because someone was clever enough to turn up the thermostat.

For this book to make a difference you have to believe that the little things really do matter and that even one of them is enough to win or lose you a game.

This book isn't about soccer technique. I'm just going to assume that since you were interested enough to purchase this book, your technique is already sound (or perhaps you're a coach). This book is about soccer decisions that take place during the course of a match — those snapshots of choices that a coach can see a player make and think, *Yeah, that kid is clever.*

These concepts are in no particular order. All of them are important and any one of them could provide your team with the margin of victory.

I've been coaching college soccer for more than 20 years and I'm amazed at how many players advance to the collegiate level without a mastery of these rudimentary concepts. They are simple. They would appear to be nothing more than common sense. But trust me, there is nothing common about the player who understands these concepts and consistently applies them during the run of play.

Mostly, this book is a collection of soccer nuggets. The value of each nugget can be big enough to win a game or even a national championship - as you will read later. But conceptually they are very basic. Most of them cannot stand alone as the basis for a training session or even a segment of a training session. They are just too small. Mainly they are bite-sized ideas that coaches can only explain to their players and then hope that when the time comes, the players remember.

I began jotting down these soccer nuggets with the idea that one year I would unveil them to my team, one per day, through the entirety of a season as the *Tip of the Day*. After a decade of intending to do that but never actually following through, I decided it would just be easier to turn them into one very easy to read book. And here it is.

Welcome to your Soccer IQ.

CHAPTER 1

THE HOLY GRAIL

Let's begin at the beginning. Speed of play. It's the Holy Grail of soccer. Understanding this is the preeminent prerequisite for becoming a smart player. Don't question why. Fast is better than slow. That's just how it is. Your job is to take everything you can already do and do it faster.

If you can embrace the idea that fast is intrinsically better than slow, you're halfway home. If you can get an entire team of players to embrace that idea, you're going to win a lot of games.

All other things being equal, if I can get the ball from Point A to Point B with one touch, it is better than getting it there in two touches. Why? Because one touch is faster than two touches, and fast is better than slow. Yes, there are exceptions and I understand that. However, too often you play as if the exception was the rule. Let me give you some wonderful advice:

- If you can get the job done with one touch, don't take two.

- If you can get it done with two touches, don't take three.

The more touches it takes you to do your job, the slower your job gets done. The challenge for an intelligent player is to do the most effective job possible in as few touches as possible. If you could take a time machine back to your last game, could you accomplish everything that you'd accomplished during that game, but with fewer touches? It would require you to think faster. It would require you to make decisions before the ball arrived. It would require you to perform with sharper technical ability. In short, it would require you to do the things that a better player would do.

Too many players don't understand the intrinsic value of moving the ball quickly. Instead of playing a quick and simple pass that will dictate a fast tempo, the simple pass becomes their last resort – after they have evaluated and exhausted all other options. Too often they feel obligated to make an impact on the score-line every time the ball is at their feet. Every time the ball finds them, they're searching to find that killer pass; trying to figure out how to win the game right then and there. And because the answer isn't always ready to reveal itself, they get caught hemming and hawing over their options as their team's speed of play methodically dies a slow death.

Slow play is the enemy. Slow play allows your opponent to get organized. Slow play leads to turnovers. Slow play loses games.

Every pass you make doesn't have to be *the* pass. *YOU* don't have to win the game every time *YOU* touch the ball. Sometimes just moving the ball to a team-mate is good enough. And moving it quickly is better than moving it slowly.

Have you seen Barcelona play? A Barcelona player will never be accused of trying to win the game each time he touches the ball – not even the prolific goal-scorer Lionel Messi. Barca's players are so patient in possession that at times they don't seem to even realize there's a goal on the field. It can look like they are just passing for passing's sake. The way they meticulously grind teams into the ground with possession has been dubbed *death by a thousand passes*. But even with all that big-picture patience, they still move the ball very quickly with a minimum of touches. So while the whole machine might be perceived as slow or deliberate, the parts are still moving at breakneck speed. Patience and speed are coexisting in stunning harmony. Barcelona's players have bought into this concept. Each player understands the value of moving the ball quickly; and each player knows that if he doesn't have the answer when the ball gets to his feet, the teammate he passes to just might. At Barcelona, speed of play is the culture.

It will also behoove you to understand soccer's speed ladder:

Slowest – A player dribbling the ball while making lateral movements and fakes.

Slow – A player running with the ball, straight ahead, at top speed.

Faster – A player running without the ball

Fastest – A moving ball

Nothing on the soccer field is faster than a moving ball. Nothing. The fastest player on the field cannot cover ten yards as fast as a kicked ball. Neither can you. And this is where you have to make a choice between taking superfluous touches that accomplish nothing more than momentarily indulging your ego...

and winning. If you want to move the ball twenty yards, you'll be able to do it much faster if you pass it rather than dribble it. And fast is better than slow.

Let me add this invaluable tidbit of wisdom: To play fast, you have to *want* to play fast. It is a decision you have to make before the game begins. You've got to consciously decide to play fast. You've got to consciously decide to limit your touches. Playing fast doesn't happen by accident. It's not going to happen unless you actually decide to make it happen.

Speed of play is more than a habit – it's a lifestyle. And you can't live it until you internalize and embrace the concept that nothing is more important than speed of play. Fast is better than slow. Speed of play is what wins games. Smart players prioritize playing quickly.

Note for Coaches: It's amazing how well our team can play when we apply a one-touch restriction to a training exercise. It can be a glorious sight when our players ping the ball around at breakneck speed. The challenge for coaches is getting the players to translate that same speed of play to a match when there are no restrictions. If there is a significant difference in those two environments, then your players haven't internalized the importance of playing fast for its own sake. You've got to convince your players to *want* to play fast.

In Chapter 8 you'll read about one of my favorite possession games, called 31. It is an excellent exercise for helping players decipher when to play with one touch and when to hold the ball.

CHAPTER 2

PLAY FROM A SPOT

'Playing from a spot' means killing the ball close to you and then passing or shooting from that spot. It couldn't be simpler, right?

Let's say a player receives a ball at midfield facing her opponent's goal. The closest opponent is 12 yards away, directly in front of her. At this moment the player in possession has a 12-yard cushion that she can use to pick her head up and find a passing option. It would make perfect sense for her to play from a spot by killing the ball close to her body and forcing that defender to cover every inch of those 12 yards in order to threaten the ball.

Instead, the attacker takes her first touch forward four yards. The opponent has started to close ground from her end and has covered five yards. Now that 12-yard cushion has become a three-yard cushion and in half a second it will have disappeared entirely. The next thing you hear is the sound of feet colliding and a ball bouncing haphazardly to the opposing team.

I am amazed at how many players play the game as if they were NFL running backs, receiving the ball and running forward with it until they get tackled. I'll never understand why a player would voluntarily concede that cushion between her and the defender. That cushion is your time. It is your time to make a good decision and to execute technique under a minimal amount of pressure. Why would you willingly surrender that?

When you take that lengthy first touch toward your opponent, you're doing half her work for her! It's not your job to bring the ball closer to her. It's her job to cover the ground to pressure you. Stop doing your opponent's job! Stop making *her* life easier and *yours* harder!

When you kill the ball close to you, you put yourself in a position to immediately play forward. This gives the closing defender a new problem because now, instead of worrying about tackling the ball from your foot, her primary consideration becomes stopping your forward pass. Instead of focusing on charging at you, now she must prepare her body to move side to side to block your pass. In effect, when you set your body to play the ball forward, you freeze the defender and preserve your cushion. This is a good thing.

What confounds me even more is how often a player will plow through that cushion before she even has control of the ball. Every time I watch a club game I see players running the ball down the field while it is bouncing off their knees and shins and thighs and stomachs. Exactly what are you expecting to accomplish when you haven't even gotten the ball down to the ground? For Pete's sake, take a breath and get the ball on the deck! First things first, right? Trust me, you're better off putting on the brakes and getting control of the ball before embarking on your sixty-yard run for glory.

When I explain the play-from-a-spot concept to a team I'll use a video from an English Premier League game. It doesn't matter what game. Every EPL game will illustrate the point because every Premier League team has smart players who understand the value of not putting oneself under undo pressure. At the professional level, especially when in their defensive or middle thirds of the field, players will habitually receive a pass and kill the ball close to them. Their next touch is usually an unpressured pass to a teammate.

I encourage you to watch one half of an EPL game and count how many times both teams play from a spot (One-touch passes also qualify as playing from a spot.). Then watch one of your own games and count the same thing. There's a reason your team gives the ball away so much. There's a reason you rarely see a youth team string more than three passes in a row. It's because the players haven't mastered this very simple concept. You can't expect to maintain possession of the ball when you are constantly running yourself into pressure.

Learn to play from a spot. You will complete a lot more of your passes and your team will spend much more time in possession of the ball.

Note for Coaches: If you understand this, get your players to understand it also. It will make an immediate impact on your team's ability to keep possession of the ball. I suggest the video exercise mentioned above. Divide your team into two groups. Watch one half of an EPL game. Assign each group to one of the EPL teams. Have each group chart the number of play-from-a-spot passes that its EPL team makes. If you want to really hammer home the point, follow the EPL game with a video of one of your own games and again chart the play-from-a-spot passes. I promise you that the staggering statistical difference will make an impact on your players.

CHAPTER 3

THE IMPOSSIBLE PASS

I've never been satisfied by the on-field communication of my players. If I could ever get all of them to generously communicate useful information during the run of play, we would rise to a whole new and improved level. But more about that later. This chapter isn't just about what to say; it's about what *not* to say, and when *not* to say it.

Smart players that communicate well talk about what's best for the ball. They feed their teammates a concise stream of information that helps those teammates solve their soccer problems. They are like chess-masters moving the pieces to orchestrate the attack, directing the ball from one teammate to the next. That's what smart players do.

What most players do is see the teammate who has the ball and then scream, "JENNY! JENNY! JENNY!"

And there's poor Jenny at midfield, trying her best to evade two determined opponents and the only help she's offered is ten teammates shouting her name from ten different directions. Listen – Jenny already knows her name. What Jenny needs is some useful information that will help her out of her current unpleasant predicament. Jenny needs a teammate saying something like, "Drop it to Danielle." That's the kind of information she can actually use. Instead she gets, "JENNY! JENNY! JENNY!"

The communication habits of most players are poor for one of two reasons – they don't talk enough or they don't talk smart. And players whose sole method of communication is shouting the name of the teammate with the ball are not smart talkers.

The most egregious of these offenses inspired me to create the term The Impossible Pass.

There's Jenny on the ball again. This time she's pinned up against the sideline by an opponent who is absolutely hounding her. The ball is between Jenny and the sideline. Jenny is between the opponent and the ball. And twenty yards to the other side of the opponent, there you are screaming, "JENNY! JENNY! JENNY!"

There you are, asking a teammate who is under pressure, who is not even facing you, to maneuver that ball so it can magically pass through her own body and then through that of the opponent and then carry the twenty yards to arrive at your waiting foot.

So here's my question: *How on earth do you expect her to do that?*

Look, I don't care how wide open you are. I don't care how you are guaranteed to score a goal when you receive that pass. None of that matters because JENNY CAN'T GET THAT BALL TO YOU! Get it? You are asking for an IMPOSSIBLE PASS! And the only thing your shouting will accomplish is to cloud the flow of useful information someone else might actually be trying to give her.

I understand you want the ball. I really do. But please apply some common sense to the problem. Your team is much better served if you communicate to Jenny some information that will solve the problem at hand. Maybe your useful communication will get the ball to a teammate who can then get it to you so you can go score that goal. Doesn't that make more sense?

When you talk to your teammates, speak in clear, concise words, phrases and sentences. Talk to the person on the ball as if she is blindfolded and is completely dependent upon you. Jenny doesn't know what you're thinking when you scream her name, but she'll know exactly what you mean when you say, "Man on!" or "Time" or "Turn." If she's about to cross the ball and you shout, "Near!", she'll know you want the ball served to the near post. All of these options provide Jenny with information that will help her solve her problem. Shouting Jenny's name at her won't do much good at all.

In short, don't say stupid stuff. And don't ask for the Impossible Pass. It's not coming.

Note for Coaches: Demand useful communication from your players in every possible exercise. It's amazing how much easier soccer is when players are giving and receiving useful information.

CHAPTER 4

PASSING ANGLES AND EMPATHY

Here's the thing about passing angles... being able to quickly and consistently identify proper passing angles won't make you a great player, but you will never be a great player until you can quickly and consistently identify proper passing angles.

A passing angle is a seam that runs between players (usually opponents), or between players and boundaries, that the ball can travel through without being intercepted or deflected. When a player receives the ball, there is always a seam (unless she is completely surrounded). A teammate who wants the ball must work to receive the ball in one of these seams. Because soccer is a fluid game, these seams are constantly moving - appearing, disappearing and reappearing. A smart player can read the flow of bodies between her and the ball to identify the seams that give the ball-carrier the best chance of passing her the ball and (this is the important part) she will *work* to get into one of those seams.

When it comes to what we value on the field, nothing ranks higher than speed of play. The ability to move the ball faster than the opposition can run and organize itself is the surest way to carve up the opponent. Moving the ball quickly depends on the player receiving the ball making quick decisions. That player's ability to make quick decisions depends on the options available to her as the ball arrives. Those options are entirely predicated upon her teammates' ability to quickly identify and move into passing seams.

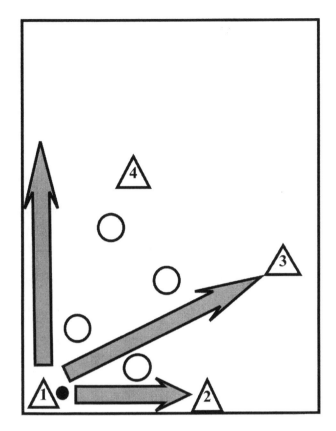

Diagram 4.1 – The attacker on the ball has 3 available seams. Attackers #2 and #3 have gotten into two of those seams, but Attacker #4 is hiding in dead space behind two defenders.

We frequently want our players to play with one touch. A player cannot do that if she doesn't have teammates giving her useful options, particularly in the direction she is facing. But if at least one teammate can get into a useful seam in that direction, the player can receive and pass the ball in a single touch. And there is no faster speed of play than one-touch passing.

Sounds simple, right? Well in theory it is. But watch any possession exercise and you'll see countless examples of players who get anchored in dead space instead of working to get into a seam. And because of that you'll see countless examples of a team losing the ball when it absolutely didn't have to lose it.

Identifying a seam should be easy. It takes one solitary quality – *empathy*. Empathize with the teammate who is about to receive the ball. Ask yourself, "If I was her, and I wanted to play with one touch, where would I want my teammate to be?" Well, you wouldn't want her hiding behind opponents. You'd want her in a seam that ran between opponents. Identifying that seam is Step 1.

Step 2 is actually moving your feet to get into that seam. The only question you need to ask yourself now is whether or not you actually want the ball, because you're not going to get it if you're hiding behind an opponent. The ball can't travel through opponents, but it can sure as heck travel through that seam. If you want the ball, make your teammate's life easy and get into that seam.

Note for Coaches: Don't be afraid to stop your possession exercises every single time a player gives a passing angle that is less than perfect. You've got to be willing to hammer away at this point day after day after day. Just because a player understands where to go, it doesn't automatically mean that she'll go there. You've got to drive this point home.

CHAPTER 5

RECEIVING WITH THE PROPER FOOT

Once you've identified and moved into the proper seam, the next part is making that tiny, little extra effort to make sure the ball comes to your proper foot, which is normally going to be the foot furthest from the defender who will be pressuring the pass you receive.

As you advance to higher levels of soccer, merely getting into the proper seam isn't enough. You must also understand what foot needs to be the one receiving the ball. You need to have decisions made before the ball gets to you and those decisions will dictate which foot should be the one receiving the ball.

When deciding which foot to receive the ball with you must ask yourself these questions:

Which foot will help me escape pressure?

Which foot will help me advance the ball?

Which foot will set up my next pass?

And by all means, don't take that first touch into pressure. Be prepared to receive the ball and immediately put your body between the ball and the pressuring defender.

Regardless of which foot receives the ball, remember that you don't always get to take two touches. There's no rule that says you're entitled to settle every ball that comes to you. Be prepared to play with a single touch, because often times, that's all you're going to get. If you don't have the necessary time and space to settle the ball, don't pretend that you do. Make the adjustment and play with one-touch.

The ability to make these adjustments can literally mean the margin of victory to your team.

Note for Coaches: Players who receive the ball with the wrong foot either don't know what they're doing wrong or they're being lazy. The only way to make this a habit is to demand perfection during training sessions. Details matter.

CHAPTER 6

PASSING TO THE PROPER FOOT

In Chapter 5 you were the player hoping to receive the ball. Now you're the player with the ball and your next move is to pass it to a teammate.

Again you must remember the value of speed of play. And you have to set up your teammate so that she too can play quickly or at the very least have a fighting chance of keeping possession of the ball. And that means passing the ball to her proper foot.

Soccer is full of little big things and this is one of them. It's astonishing how many potentially great attacks are not stymied by the opponent but rather by one of our own players passing the ball to the wrong foot. Here's an example:

Our center midfielder angles her dribble toward our right wing setting up a 2v1 against the opponent's left back (see Diagram 6.1). The midfielder's job is to commit the left back and then pass it by her to our right wing who is standing against the sideline. The midfielder does exactly as she's been coached to do. The left back commits and our midfielder pushes the ball past her. If the pass arrives at our winger's right foot, she can take an explosive first touch down the line to create separation from the defender. Unfortunately the pass is to our winger's left foot. Now she has to take a half-step back to collect the ball and before she can take a second touch, the defender has recovered and our winger is forced to play backwards so we can keep possession and our once promising attack has stalled and we have to start over.

A foot and a half - that's all we're talking about here. That pass was off by a mere 18 inches and yet it ruined a perfectly good chance to create a goal-scoring opportunity. Little things, yes?

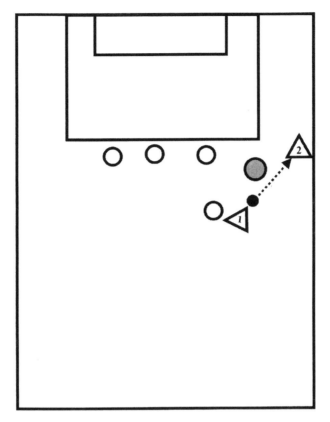

**If the attacker engages the outside back (shaded) and passes to the winger's for-
ward foot, the winger can take her first touch in behind the defender. If the pass
arrives at her trailing foot, the winger will not be able to penetrate with her first
touch.**

When you're on the ball you have to empathize with the teammate who will
receive it and you have to give her the best chance to be successful. Sometimes
it's so obvious that it's literally painful. If you pass it to your teammate's left foot
she can protect it from the opponent who is closing her down. But if you play it
to her right foot it becomes a 50-50 ball and your teammate gets clobbered by
a thundering tackle.

Here's an example from a recent training session with a player I'll call Jackie
Jones. We were playing 5v5+GKs and Jackie received the ball, back to goal at
the penalty spot. Jackie had heavy pressure on her so she decided to lay the ball
back to her wide-open teammate, Meghan. Meghan hit a first-time shot from 22

yards that she shanked wide. At that point I stopped training and this conversation followed:

> DB: Jackie, how long have you known Meghan?
> JJ: 3 Years.
> DB: And can you tell me what her strong foot is?
> JJ: Her left.
> DB: So why did you pass the ball to her right foot?
> JJ: Because I'm an idiot.

Okay, Jackie is by no means an idiot, but her pass was in fact idiotic. Meghan is one of the best strikers of the ball I've ever seen... *with her left foot.* Jackie knew that, but didn't put enough thought into her pass for it to do her team any good. At our level this is an unacceptable mental error.

To play at a higher level you've got to hold yourself to a higher standard. Merely getting the ball to your teammate is no longer good enough. You've got to put her in the best possible position and that means delivering the proper ball to her proper foot. Here's a really simple way to remember it: *Give a pass that you'd like to receive.* Don't bounce it into your teammate if you can just as easily keep the ball on the ground. Don't smash it at her abdomen when you can pass it to her feet. And don't pass it to her right foot if she needs it on her left.

Let me give you one other piece of advice about these passes: When that ball comes off your foot, until it arrives at your teammate, it is *your* responsibility. If it doesn't reach its intended target, no one is going to blame the target. So if your teammate hasn't given you an adequate passing angle, don't pretend she has. Too often I see players try to force the ball into a teammate who has given an unacceptable angle and time after time after time that pass quickly becomes the opponent's ball.

If the angle she gives you isn't good enough, *don't pass the ball to her.* And if you must pass the ball to her, then don't aim for where she is. Play your pass to where she is supposed to be. Pass to the acceptable angle and let her go get it. Trust me, it's a lot easier for your team to keep the ball that way.

I once coached a center back who was constantly irritated at our right back for giving lazy passing angles. No matter how many times we rehearsed it in training, when we played a match, the right back simply refused to give an acceptable passing angle. She was always asking for a high-risk pass that had the chance of being intercepted by the opposing forward. One game our center back finally got fed up with her lazy teammate. So as we switched fields from left to right, our center back would intentionally put her pass twenty yards behind the right back, forcing her to run and retrieve it. After a few games of this the right back demanded to know why the center back kept giving her bad passes. The center back snapped at her, "When you start giving me good angles, I'll start giving you good passes." Amen.

Note for Coaches: At Georgia, we hound our players about passing to the proper foot because it is an essential detail to smart soccer. If a player passes to the wrong foot in a possession game, we're going to let her know about it. In some of our exercises, passing the ball to the wrong foot is an automatic forfeiture of possession.

CHAPTER 7

LIFTING THE TIGHT-ANGLE PASS

There are going to be times when you will need to play a pass along a very tight angle. If you pass it on the ground, the defender will stick a toe out and deflect away the ball. In these situations, lift your pass about twelve inches off the ground. The ball will go over the crook in the defender's outstretched foot and reach its destination. You can regularly see high-level players implementing this technique.

Note for Coaches: A great opportunity for discussing this pass is during 3v1 possession drills because the players will frequently find themselves having to pass along a tight angle.

CHAPTER 8

THE THREE-STEP RULE

When your team has possession you are either the player with the ball or one of the ten players who can potentially help her. And often times you can (and should) go from one of these roles to the other and back again in a matter of seconds.

As soon as that ball leaves your foot, you've got to switch roles. You must immediately transition from being the passer to being a passing option, which is why smart players follow the three-step rule.

Normally, when you make a pass, a defender is going to chase the ball. When she chases, she will move into the ball's wake, as if the ball were pulling her along by a string. Her movement into that path means that she has put herself between you and the person about to receive the ball, and that leaves you in dead space. Thankfully there's an easy fix. Normally, getting out of dead space is a matter of taking three steps to either side. Take these three steps quickly enough and again you become a viable passing option for your teammate.

We run possession games with the three-step rule. Anytime a player passes the ball, she must immediately take at least three steps to give a better passing angle. If she doesn't, we stop the game and award possession of the ball to the opposing team.

For smart players, for players who want the ball, three steps (at least) is a very valuable habit.

Note for Coaches: Try this possession exercise. It's called 31 and it's my favorite because it incorporates so many aspects of possession, including when to play one-touch and when to take two or more touches. It's a tough one to keep track of, so if you have some helpers or injured players available (preferably 3), call them into service and assign a team to each one of them.

Divide your group into three teams of four and use a grid about 30 x20 yards. Adjust the size of the grid as necessary. One team is yellow, another is blue, and the third team is red. To start, red and blue play keep-away from yellow. If the blue team, for example, gives the ball away or knocks it out of bounds, the red and yellow immediately play keep-away from blue. There is no touch restriction, but whenever a player on either of the two attacking teams successfully passes the ball to any other attacking player with one touch, *both* attacking teams are credited with a point. To clarify, two teams get credit for every point that is scored. The object of the game is to be the first team to score 31 points.

CHAPTER 9

BETTER THAN SQUARE

In earlier chapters we discussed being empathetic with the teammate who is receiving the ball and making her life easier by providing her with an excellent angle of support. In Diagram 9.1, the target forward for Δ is about to receive a pass, under pressure, with her back to goal. The supporting teammate must choose an angle of support that makes the target's life as easy as possible for a one-touch layoff.

Too often the supporting player runs past the target player as the ball arrives at the target's feet. When she runs past the target player, there is no easy way (and often times no way at all) for the target to deliver her the ball. Common sense says that the ball can't magically pass through the defender's body, so barring some type of miraculous flick-on, the supporting teammate has run herself out of any useful position.

Remember, it's always easiest to play the way you face. That also applies to your teammates. If you want to provide a useful angle of support, you can't run past the player on the ball. You have got to give her the opportunity to play the way she's facing. And just because you haven't run completely past her, it doesn't necessarily mean you've given her a good angle. When the angle of support you give her requires a perfectly square lay-off, you haven't made her life much easier.

Often times, when the ball arrives at the target's feet, the supporting player has gone so high up the field that only a square pass - an absolutely flawless square pass lay-off – will do the trick. This is better than running past the target, but only slightly. The target can play the way she's facing, but just barely, and you've given her no margin for error whatsoever. She has to play a perfect ball that keeps you perfectly in stride and that's an awful lot of perfection to ask of anyone. If the timing of her layoff is skewed by even one millisecond, you will overrun her pass. And once you overrun it, you're not going to be able to stop, turn around and retrieve it. That play has died and the opponent has taken the ball. Additionally, even if your teammate does play the perfect square pass, the pressuring defender may have an opportunity to reach a toe out and deflect it before it reaches you.

The simple solution here is to put on the brakes and give her a bigger angle. Instead of flying by the target and asking her to do something remarkable, just slow down and hold your run and support underneath her so she can play the way she is facing. Give her an angle of support that is better than square. Give her some margin for error. Make her life easy. *Empathy*, remember?

If you stop underneath her, her layoff doesn't have to be perfect – it just has to be decent. All she has to do is lay the ball down somewhere in front of you. You can always come forward to adjust to her pass. And because you've stopped underneath the target, she can shield the defender that's on her back to buy you an extra second of time on the ball.

Another common mistake the supporting player makes in this situation is not reading the side of the target's body to which the initial entry pass will arrive. If you are supporting wide of the target and the entry pass is to her inside foot, then you need to adjust your angle and move further inside. You've got to be able to see the pass and read the target's body language. Don't ask her to take a ball that's on one side of her body and turn it back across to the other side of her body with one touch. Remember, as the supporting player your job is to make your teammate's life as easy as possible. All it really takes is putting yourself in the target's shoes and asking, "If I were her, where would I want my support to be." Then get there fast.

Note for Coaches: This is one of those easy-to-fix problems that will give you fits if it goes unchecked. I started using the phrase "better than square" a few years ago and found it has that memorable quality that will stick with players.

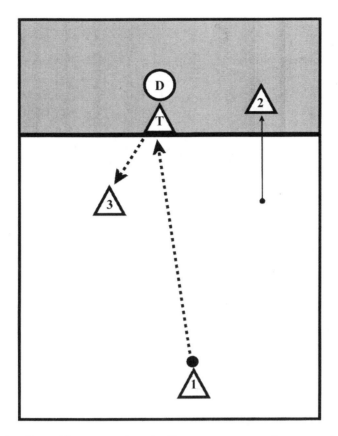

Diagram 9.1 – The white area below the Target represents the space that is better than square. As the Target receives the ball with pressure on her back, Attacker #2 has run herself out of a useful supporting angle by running beyond the Target. Attacker #3 offers support in a useful spot underneath the Target. She has made the Target's job easier by allowing her to play the way she is facing and providing her with some margin for error.

CHAPTER 10

THREE QUESTIONS

What if? What's next? What's behind me? These three questions will change your soccer life.

Whenever I coach at soccer camp I always ask my players what a soccer player's most important body part is. As you might expect, the most common answer is, "Your feet!" And it may be what you answered also. Well, the campers are wrong.

A soccer player's most important body part is her pair of eyes. Your eyes are your very best way of collecting information. They are your cameras. They are what you use to take film. Your eyes prepare you to make the decisions that enable you to play quickly and keep the ball for your team. And too many players don't utilize them very well.

In a ninety minute soccer game you will probably spend between two and three minutes on the ball. That means that 87 minutes, roughly 96% of your day, is spent off the ball. Smart players understand that when they don't have the ball, they've got to plan for those moments when the ball finds them. And the easiest and most effective way to make those plans is to use your eyes. And I'm not talking about seeing what's in front of you. That's the easy part. That's the part you can't miss. I'm talking about knowing what's going on behind you. Because behind you is where danger lurks and opportunity beckons.

A smart player is constantly asking herself, "What if?" and "What's next?"
What if the ball comes to me?
What's next when I get it?
What if we give the ball back to them? What's next?
What if they give the ball back to us? What's next?
And she is always asking, "What's behind me?"

Average soccer players make their decisions after they've already received the ball. That's not a good thing. For starters, it makes it impossible to play one-touch soccer. Secondly, it invites tackles from opponents. And thirdly, it will paralyze your attack from slow play.

Smart players make 90% of their decisions before the ball ever gets to them. Even if that decision is to face up a defender and take her on the dribble, the smart player already knows that's what she's going to do before the ball gets to her.

Now here's the thing – soccer is a fluid game and your decisions are subject to change at a moment's notice and that's both fine and necessary. But the smart player will at least have Plan A in mind before the ball ever gets to her. If the picture changes, she can always go to Plan B. But the smart player knows at least one option before she ever gets the ball. And often times that option is behind her.

You've got to know what's behind you. As a defender, you can't let clever forwards sneak in behind you. As a player in possession, you have to know what your best options are and you have to be aware of the blindside opponent who wants to knock you into next week. Smart players are constantly taking film. They keep their head on a swivel, constantly evaluating their options and their opponent's options. Coaches often refer to this as *checking your shoulder*.

If you think you already do this at an acceptable level, then let me ask you this: When was the last time you dummied the ball to a teammate during a game? Dummies aren't just for sizzle. They can be a tremendously effective weapon. But you hardly ever see them, even at the college level, because very few players are keenly aware of what is going on behind them. In twenty years of coaching college soccer I doubt I've seen ten dummy passes.

When asking, *"What if,"* becomes a habit for you, you will naturally keep your head on a swivel and your game will improve dramatically. It's amazing how much easier soccer is when you know what's going on around you and behind you and when you have a plan before you have the ball.

Note for Coaches: Whenever we do exercises that prioritize speed of play (everything from possession games to full-field scrimmages), you can always hear me shouting, *"What's next! What if the ball comes to you!"* I shout these phrases incessantly because I want my players to internalize those thoughts into their own brains. I find that it gets our team playing with more urgency and increases our speed of play.

If you have a player who struggles with this concept, have her take it one training session at a time. Before each session have her set a goal for that day's scrimmage to keep her head on a swivel. When she realizes how much easier the game becomes, checking her shoulder will become a habit.

CHAPTER 11

THE UNABOMBER PASS

The Unabomber Pass is one that no teammate wants to receive because it puts them on the wrong end of a 40-60 ball. It's the equivalent of leaving a mail bomb at her feet.

It typically begins when the player on the ball finds herself with a little extra time and space. She sees a teammate, Option A, and considers passing it to her. Option A is 20 yards away from her nearest opponent, so if that pass is played quickly, everything is peachy because Option A will have time on the ball and the chance to do something productive. But of course that's too darn easy.

Although Option A is a very logical choice, the ball-carrier is swayed by the abundance of time she thinks she has (and assumes her teammates will have also) and decides to peruse her other options. She evaluates Option B but decides against it. She then considers Option C and realizes that's no good either. Having concluded that Options B and C aren't wise choices and now faced with pressure herself, she decides to finally play the pass to Option A. The problem is that in the matter of seconds it took the ball-carrier to evaluate her choices and pass the ball, the opponent who was initially 20 yards away from Option A is now only five yards away and bearing down on her like a freight train. When the ball finally arrives at Option A's feet, it is met by a thunderous tackle. Option A gets blown up – thus the Unabomber Pass.

To recap, had the ball-carrier made the sound choice to immediately pass to her open teammate, her team would still have the ball and her teammate wouldn't be laid out on the ground picking grass out of her teeth. Instead, the ball-carrier's slow play allowed the opponent to close ground and put her teammate in a very compromising position. Coaches are always saying, "Keep it simple." This is a perfect example of what happens when you complicate matters.

At the Division I college level, the average player can run the entire length of a 120 yard field in 16 seconds. Using a little oversimplified math we can assume that same player can cover 60 yards in eight seconds and 30 yards in four seconds. My point is this: it doesn't take long at all for an opponent to cover 10-20 yards so when your teammate is available, *pass her the darn ball!* When she wants the ball, give it to her! You're not doing your team any good by dwelling on the ball for an extra two seconds. When I see this happen I want to ask the ball carrier what good she felt she was doing our team by holding onto that ball. How does waiting those extra two seconds possibly benefit us? If you're going to pass it to her anyway, why not just pass it to her quickly when she's in a position to do something productive with it? Why would you wait just long enough to get your teammate killed?

I've even seen examples where the ball carrier in the above scenario, under pressure from an opponent, dribbles 15 of those 20 yards before releasing a five-yard pass. Now the teammate receiving the ball is under immediate pressure from the same opponent who was hounding the original ball-carrier. With that five-yard pass the original ball-carrier is basically saying, "I don't want this girl to tackle me so I'm going to give you the ball and let her tackle you."

Smart players make the ball do what's best for the team. They aren't ego-bound to hold onto the ball for an extra second or two. They understand that their passes should put their teammates in the best possible position to be successful. And more often than not that means playing quickly and simply and not burying teammates under the weight of a Unabomber Pass.

Note for Coaches: This is a battle you will fight forever. As we discussed in Chapter 1, often times the reason players play slowly is that they desperately want to have an impact on the game every time they touch the ball and that can lead to slow decisions. And slow decisions lead to slow play. I try to teach players that they don't have to win the game for us every time they touch the ball. There's an inherent value to possessing the ball, moving it quickly and making the opponent chase. Your players need to understand that sometimes just keeping the ball for your team is good enough.

CHAPTER 12

GET PROACTIVE

Smart forwards are exceptionally easy to spot at the youth level because they stick out like sore thumbs.

Do you want to know the fundamental difference between a smart forward and every other forward? When playing in advance of the ball, the average forward drifts around the field until she sees where the ball is kicked and then reacts and tries to chase it down. The average forward is reactive.

The smart forward is *proactive* and runs to the place where she wants the ball delivered. She may want it at her feet; she may want it in space behind the defense; she may want it wide or up the middle. But no matter where she wants it, her running communicates her desires to her teammate on the ball.

Your teammates may be wonderful and talented but they are not psychic. They can't read your mind. If your running does not tell them where to pass the ball, they'll never know. You need to be proactive in your running. Your proactive runs let your teammate know where she should play the ball. You need to make it so the ball can find you and not the other way around.

Smart forwards are proactive and they let their teammates know where and when they want the ball.

Note for Coaches: Some players have a natural feel for the game and just seem to know where to run. But most don't. And that's why most forwards are reactive and not proactive. If a player isn't naturally proactive, chances are it's because she doesn't know where to run and ends up paralyzed. You may have to use a two part solution. The first step is just getting her to run somewhere, even if she's not making the best possible runs. Once she's in the habit of running proactively, then she'll begin to figure out where to run. Video is a great tool to show the good and bad examples of this concept. In Chapter 16 you'll find one of my favorite exercises, the Endzone Game. This is a very effective game to produce smart, proactive runs in advance of the ball.

CHAPTER 13

THE UNWINNABLE RACE

Okay, so you're a forward. Your center midfielder is advancing the ball up the field on the dribble. The line of defenders is retreating and while everything is happening at breakneck speed, you've got to decide where you want the ball and then communicate that information to the ball-carrier.

As the line of defenders retreats, the defender responsible for neutralizing you has a seven-yard cushion on you and is dropping toward her goal.

Do you know why I'm writing this chapter?

Because too many times you ask for that ball to be played in *behind* that defender!

Okay, you may be fast, but let's face it — you aren't strapped to a patriot missile. And as badly as you want to be in behind that defense dribbling at the goalkeeper, that defender has too big of a head-start on you. *You can't win that race!*

So as a smart player, you go to Plan B. You put on the brakes, maybe check back two steps and ask for the ball at your feet where you actually have a chance to receive it. Doesn't that make more sense?

There's no point in putting yourself into footraces that you can't possibly win. Evaluate the situation and then demonstrate some common sense. If you can get in behind the defense, that's fantastic and you should go for it! But wishing won't make it so. If it's not on, *it's not on*. Don't be afraid to change your plan to adapt to the situation.

Whether you're the player who might ask for the ball into the space behind the defense, or the teammate who might decide to play that ball, there are two other considerations that should factor into your decision. The first is the pure physical speed of the player asking to be on the receiving end. If that player is of average pace, perhaps she isn't the best candidate to volunteer for footraces. And secondly, you must consider the amount of field that remains behind the opponent's line of defenders. Even if the attacker can win the race against her defender, there is also the matter of the goalkeeper who will be charging from her line to shorten the field from the other end. Before orchestrating an attack based on a through-ball, make sure there is enough field remaining behind the defenders to give your team a realistic chance of producing something dangerous. This is particularly true if the necessary ball must be played up the middle of the park where the goalkeeper's presence is more prominent.

Note for Coaches: Even if it was your forward who initiated the unwinnable race, the midfielder who played her the ball is equally culpable for the headache you're experiencing. She's got to recognize the futility of the situation and find a different option. Video is a phenomenally effective tool for dissecting these moments.

CHAPTER 14

TWO RUNS

Sometimes you want the ball in behind. Sometimes you want it at your feet. Sometimes you want it to your left foot, sometimes to your right. Regardless of where you want the ball to be played, it's critically important that your teammate on the ball knows where you want her to play the ball.

This was a major sticking point early in the 2010 season for our team at Georgia. The forwards were vague in their communication about where they wanted the ball so our midfielders' passes were often being intercepted or met by clattering tackles. Our forwards had to learn to pull back from defenders if they wanted it at their feet and to get on their horse if they wanted it in behind.

Some of the best soccer advice I ever got was this: *Two runs. One run for the defender's benefit, one for mine.* That means that once you determine where you want the ball, take your first two or three steps in the opposite direction. Want it at your feet? First check away. Want it behind the defense? Come back to the ball first and then spin out. Those first few decoy steps buy you the space you want.

If your defender is giving you a big cushion, don't worry about getting behind her. Use the opportunity to set her up for later in the game. Sprint a couple of steps at her to run her off, then as she retreats, quickly put on the brakes, check back to the ball and ask for it at your feet. Do this enough times and she'll stop giving you that cushion. When she starts cheating too far forward, ask for that ball in behind.

Once you determine where you want the ball, be crystal clear in your communication to your teammate with the ball. Tell her, "Feet!" Point to the foot where you want the ball. Point to the space in behind where you want the ball. But take all of the mystery out of her decision by letting her know as plainly as possible where you want her to pass the ball.

Note for Coaches: I think the decoy run is the most difficult thing to teach a player in all of soccer. Most players just don't understand the benefit of making an extra run or they have no concept of how to time it or they're just too darn lazy to actually do it. If you can get even half of your players to habitually initiate decoy runs during game situations, give yourself a pat on the back.

CHAPTER 15

DOES SHE NEED ME?

A lot of your running in advance of the ball must be determined by the pressure on the ball-carrier. As we learned in Chapter 3, The Impossible Pass, it doesn't matter how wide open you are if the ball-carrier can't possibly deliver you the ball.

When your midfielder has received the ball and turned to face the defense, you've got to evaluate the situation very quickly. Keeping in mind that the situation can and will change in two or three seconds, the question you have to ask yourself is very simple: *Does she need me?*

Your answer will be determined by the amount of pressure on the ball-carrier. If she's not under pressure, she'll have the chance to pick her head up, get balanced and play a bigger ball. If she is under pressure, there's a much greater likelihood that she won't be able to get comfortably balanced and see down the field so she'll have to play a shorter pass.

If the ball-carrier is not under immediate pressure and the defense isn't giving you too big of a cushion, then your first look should be to see if you can receive the ball in behind the defense. If the ball-carrier is about to be put under pressure, then she probably needs you to come back and ask for the ball at your feet.

If you've watched some NFL games, then you've heard the commentators talk about a scrambling quarterback. To throw the ball far down the field, the quarterback must be able to set his feet and get balanced. When a quarterback is being chased out of the pocket he doesn't have the chance to set his feet, so the receivers are expected to break off their routes and come back to the ball. Same goes for soccer. When she needs help, go back to her and make her life easier.

Note for Coaches: When your forwards understand this and can apply it during matches, you're going to start scoring a lot more goals. This is another topic where video will be very useful.

CHAPTER 16

THE SPLITS

Defenders love forwards that run straight up and down the field like they are on train tracks. Those forwards are predictable. They don't give defenders any difficult choices to make and that makes a defender's job very easy. But forwards who are mobile and interchange positions and run across defensive zones force defenders into all types of decisions. Not only that, but they force defenders into communicating. And the more you force defenders to make decisions and to communicate, the more likely they are to screw it up.

The most dangerous pass in soccer is a penetrating ball that splits a pair of defenders, often referred to as a seam ball or a split. That's why smart defenses are set up to prevent this pass at all costs. But that doesn't mean it's never available. And when it's on, you want to take advantage of it!

Smart players recognize when they've caught a defense flat and when a seam exists that allows for a ball that will split the defense. And when that moment beckons, they make a slashing, diagonal run across defensive zones. The hope is that the attacker will travel through one seam, the ball will travel through another, and they will meet up behind the defense.

This is, by and large, the most difficult pass in soccer which is more reason to celebrate its effectiveness. It takes communication and timing and precise technical execution on the passer's part. The runner must time her run so that when the ball is played, she's onsides and at a sprint as she reaches the line of defenders. And when all that comes together, chances are you have created a very dangerous goal-scoring opportunity.

At UGA we have a handbook for our defenders. So dangerous is the seam ball that on page one of our book is this commandment: *We don't get split. Not Ever. Never.* That's how much we respect the danger a seam ball will produce. It's the one pass we will not concede.

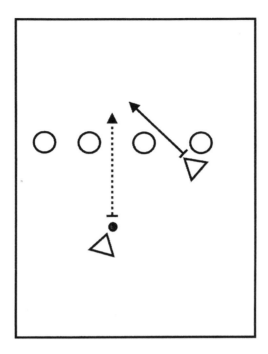

Diagram 16.1 - The Seam Ball. With the defensive line caught flat, the ball-carrier plays a seam ball that splits the two central defenders. The attacker in advance of the ball runs through a second seam and will meet up with the ball behind the defensive line. This is an extremely effective pass for creating goal-scoring chances, but the passer must make absolutely certain that the ball gets beyond the line of defenders.

Smart players know the effectiveness of the diagonal run and the seam ball that splits defenders.

Note for Coaches: One of the most common ways that the player on the ball messes this up is by trying to squeeze the ball into the same seam as the runner. More often than not that seam is too tight to accommodate both pieces. A good rule of thumb is that the ball goes through one seam while the runner goes through the other. The passer needs to play the ball to where the runner is going, not where she is. My favorite all-around exercise for playing the seam ball is the Endzone Game (Diagram 16.2).

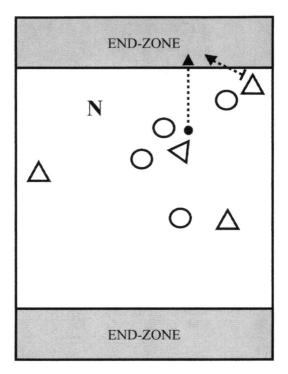

Diagram 16.2 – The End-Zone Game. 4v4 plus a Neutral player. Field is 30 yards wide by 40 yards long, plus an eight-yard end-zone at each end of the field. To score, a player must receive a pass in the end-zone, but the ball must cross into the end-zone before the player receiving it. No one from either team is allowed in the end-zones before the ball. Defenders may chase a ball into their end-zone to prevent a goal. There is no offside. Field size and number of players can be altered.

CHAPTER 17

THE BALL IN BEHIND

There are two times to play a ball in behind the opponent's defense: when it's on to create a dangerous attack, and when you have no other option. Either way, a lot of these balls fail for one simple reason – the ball never actually gets beyond the defenders.

The defensive line is like a picket fence with gaps. For a ball to get past the fence it either has to pass through one of the gaps or fly over the top of it.

When the objective is to create a dangerous attack with a pass behind the defense, the passer will often try to be too precise and leave herself no margin for error. She'll try to place that ball perfectly into her teammate's path. A sliding defender will get a toe to the ball and the attack is stifled. I've seen it a few thousand times. Sometimes you have to be perfect. But a lot of times you don't.

If that ball in behind is on, it's a golden opportunity and you can't afford to mess it up. You've got to leave yourself some margin for error and you absolutely must get that ball behind the defenders. If it gets past the defenders, at least you have a chance. The smart player understands that in those situations, the worst thing that can possibly happen is that the ball never gets beyond the defense. Then you have nothing.

When it's time for that killer ball, being precise is wonderful. But just like in horseshoes and hand grenades, being close may be good enough to get the job done.

When your teammate has gotten position on the defense, Priority #1 is giving her a chance. You don't have to be David Beckham. All you have to do is give your teammate a winnable race and a ball that she can receive facing the goal. Even if your pass isn't as good as it could be, even if it isn't a pass that poets will write sonnets about, it can still be the pass that creates a goal. And if your teammate scores, you can still post the video on Youtube.

Let's say you decide to play a ball in behind but not with the intention of orchestrating a brilliant attack. Let's just say it's because you're under some heat and you don't have any other good options and you just want to relieve pressure. It's still a great time to knock a ball in behind – under one condition – the ball actually travels beyond the line of defenders.

This was another issue we had at Georgia in 2010. Too many players were trying to be too precise, attempting to turn clearances into pinpoint passes, and instead of forcing the defenders to turn and chase the ball facing their own goal, our clearances were turning into easy headers for our opponent's back line. The reason? We just weren't kicking the ball hard enough.

The easiest part about being a defender is that 90% of the time you receive the ball facing the opponent's goal. But every defender hates chasing a ball toward her own goal with a scrappy forward bearing down on her, nipping at her heels. That's enough to rattle the best defenders.

When you decide to put the ball in behind the defensive line, make sure it gets there. Hit the darn thing! Hit it hard enough to clear the line of defenders because even if it's not perfect, it puts the defenders in an uncomfortable position and gives them a problem to solve. You have to make defenders solve problems. And if your team can turn problems into turnovers, you're going to create a lot of excellent scoring opportunities.

Clearances are like birdie putts in golf – you never want to leave them short. If you're going to err with your ball in behind, err on the side of hitting it a little bit too big, not too small.

Note for Coaches: At Georgia we solved this problem with video. First we showed examples of clearances that we hit too short and how they were an easy fix for the opponent's defenders. As fate would have it, in the next game we created a goal from a strong clearance that put the opponent's right back under pressure facing her own goal. The defender hit a lazy back-pass to the goalkeeper that one of our forwards intercepted and deposited into the net. We made sure to show that clip too.

CHAPTER 18

THE SHALLOW END

There are times when you are going to have the ball at your feet and room to run in front of you. And you are going to attack that space with gusto! You'll be in the spotlight. The crowd will stand and cheer and shout your name as you fly down the field with the promise of great things to come. Adrenaline will be surging through your veins! Then you're going to come to a wall of defenders that you can't possibly penetrate – not on the dribble, and not with a pass. You've reached a dead end. Going forward is no longer an option. What are you going to do?

At these moments the average player will get caught up in the excitement and keep plowing forward and hoping for the best. And as sure as the sun rises and sets, she will lose the ball.

Look, you've got to be realistic about what's happening around you. In the heat of the moment when everything is exciting and chaotic, you still have to keep your composure and use common sense. When the light at the end of that tunnel starts shrinking and shrinking, you've got to have the composure and the common sense to put on the brakes and turn around.

It's okay. Trust me. We understand. And we appreciate the fact that you are helping our team keep the ball as opposed to going on your own little glorified suicide mission. *We get it.*

In these moments it would behoove you to remember a lesson you learned at the swimming pool many years ago. Do you remember the first time you were in an in-ground pool, when you were just a kid and still couldn't swim? You slinked into the shallow end because it was safe there. But you wanted to test your boundaries so you would take one step after another toward the deep end. You'd let the water level come right up under your nose. Then you soon reached a spot where the water was over your head and you realized you were in danger. Then what did you do? You kicked and splashed your way back to the shallow end as fast as you possibly could. And that was a *really* good choice!

The same thing goes for soccer. You've got to realize when the water has gotten too deep and when it has, simply step on the ball and swim back toward the shallow end. Help your team keep the ball. You can't win without it.

Note for Coaches: There is not a doubt in my mind that you have players that suffer from this malady. Every team does. Here's my advice: Get it on video and show your team. Then use the swimming pool metaphor because it's memorable and easy to understand. I've literally had players shouting, "SHALLOW END!" to a teammate who was about to dribble herself into trouble. When players are reciting your metaphors, you know they stuck.

Now, contradictory to everything you've just read in this chapter, a few times in your life you may coach that very special player who can in fact occasionally dribble her way through that human wall. Don't talk her out of it. Just sit back and enjoy the show while she wins games for you.

CHAPTER 19

NO HALF-CLEARANCES

When a team of good players is constantly doing possession exercises in training, it can start to develop a dangerous habit of trying to pass its way out of every situation. And that can spell big, big trouble.

Let me be perfectly clear on this: There is a time and a place to just kick the ever-living snot out of the ball. And you can do this with your head held high without shame or remorse.

It amazes me how many times one of our defenders, standing just in front of our 18, faced with heavy pressure and a bouncing ball, will try to lob a volley into our attacking center midfielder at the bottom of the center-circle. It's a suicide ball and more times than not it ends up being jammed right back down our throat. As a defender you have got to remember your primary responsibility is to keep the opponent from scoring. Yes, we want you to keep the ball when you can, but you have to realize that there are times to cut our losses and just hoof the ball as far down the field as humanly possible. And when you do, we'll understand.

It doesn't matter what we do in training, there are times in games when we're going to lose possession of the ball. That's just soccer. The key is to lose the ball in positions that put your team in the least amount of danger. You've got to recognize those moments when it's better to definitely lose the ball in the opponent's end of the field than to possibly lose it in your own.

Watch any EPL game and you'll see a dozen massive clearances that serve no other purpose than to relieve pressure. Often it's just a matter of damage control. *If we're going to lose the ball, let's lose it as far away from our goal as possible.* Makes sense, right? Some of what we do is about making things as easy as possible for our own team. But sometimes it's just about making it as difficult as possible for our opponent. And the further they have to go to score, the more difficult their life is.

Note for Coaches: If you are a possession coach, you've got to continually remind your players that sometimes the right thing to do is to just boot the ball with everything they've got. Defenders must be constantly reminded of their priorities. Additionally, don't take clearances for granted. Like everything else in soccer, clearances are a skill. Set up sessions where your defenders see a variety of serves and have to meet them with one-touch clearances with both feet. Set up competitions where each clearance over midfield is worth a point.

CHAPTER 20

THE WORLD'S DUMBEST FOUL

A ball is played in behind the opponent's left back. She is facing her own goal, pinned against the sideline with you breathing down her neck. She shields the ball from you as she tries to figure a way out of this jam. As she shields, you are slowly and methodically forcing her back towards her own endline. As the two of you jostle, more of your teammates are closing in to crowd her. She's in one heckuva mess. Then, for no apparent reason, you lose your patience and swat the legs out from under her.

You dummy!

Why would you do that? Why? *Why, why why!*

You have every advantage you could possibly hope for. The opponent is in trouble. There's no way she can play her way out of this. Any pass she attempts to make is going to be extremely risky. The best she can hope to do is kick the ball out for a throw-in. And beyond all that, she's moving the ball closer to her own goal. She's actually doing your job for you! And what do you do? You let her off the hook with a stupid foul because you got impatient! Ugh!

Never, ever foul an opponent in that situation! Keep your composure. Stay patient. She's the one with the big problem. Make her find a way out of this mess. Don't solve the problem for her by gifting her a free-kick. Because that's just dumb.

Note for Coaches: The first time you see this in training or a game, point it out to everyone and explain why it is so important not to foul in this situation. Match video will help here, too. And if the problem persists, drop the hammer. You can't win if your players are continually letting the opponent off the hook.

CHAPTER 21

PICK A SURFACE

A low, bouncing ball is skipping straight at you. You'll have enough time to do something productive, provided your first touch is decent. So what do you do? You put your feet together, throw your arms out to the side, stand on your toes, tilt your head back, close your eyes and let the ball crash into your shin guards.

Ah yes. The dreaded double-shin trap.

My career has taken me to a level where I almost never have to deal with this anymore. And for that I am eternally thankful. Because no egregious technical ineptitude contaminates our beautiful game more completely than the insidious double-shin trap. It is a stain on our sport and for using it you should be sent to a dark room to feel shame.

Are we clear on this?

I haven't the slightest idea why anyone would choose to allow a ball to bash into her shin pads when she can just as easily present the inside of her foot to cushion the ball into a playable spot. But go to any high school soccer game and you will see it happen time after time after time. And quite frankly, you can see it at quite a few college games also.

Not everyone is a naturally gifted technical soccer player. Not every player will be able to carve up three defenders on the dribble or turn on a dime. But not every part of talent is God-given and even naturally talented players understand that you have to be at least smart enough to pick a surface to control the ball. You can't just throw yourself in front of the ball and close your eyes like you're about to take a bullet for the President. You've got to make a conscious choice to put a playable body surface behind the ball. Your job is to do more than just let it hit you and carom away. Your job is to get that ball under control and prepare it for your next pass or shot. And that won't happen if you resort to the double-shin trap.

Don't trap the ball with your shins. I really don't know how else to say it. It's just that simple. You have to demand a little bit more from yourself.

Note to Coaches: We commonly see players utilize the double-shin trap during summer soccer camps. If a camper resorts to the double-shin trap, we halt the training session and make it clear to everyone that this particular maneuver is unacceptable. High-level soccer players receive the ball with their feet, not their shins. If you want an excellent exercise to build a player's confidence and first-touch aptitude, I suggest Ping. If you aren't familiar with Ping, check out the Jan. 1, 2011 entry from my blog at www.SoccerPoet.com entitled *Making a Pro*.

CHAPTER 22

THE TOE POKE

If there is one soccer thing that youth coaches in America almost universally agree upon, it's a steadfast disapproval of the toe-ball. The toe-ball has been tagged with a nasty stigma in our country. We teach our kids not to drink, smoke, steal or kick a soccer ball with their toes. So while Brazilian strikers are gleefully scoring goals with their toes, American players treat the toe-ball like it's a disease.

Okay, the toe can't be the only or most frequently used club in your bag. It shouldn't be your signature skill because it definitely has its weaknesses. But like pretty much everything in soccer, there's a time and a place.

The toe-ball is particularly effective when you are in a mad rush - like when you are standing six yards in front of the goal and you are a quarter-second away from being destroyed by a defender and you absolutely must get that shot off. But the ball is too close to your feet so you think you need a prep touch to get it out from underneath you. This is a fantastic time to break out the toe-ball.

The advantage of the toe-poke is that it takes almost no prep time. You don't need to adjust your body. You don't need a big backswing or follow-through. When the ball is lying in front of you and you need to get rid of it immediately, why not try the old toe-banger method? Because when that ball goes into the goal, it's still worth just as much as a diving header or a bicycle kick. Incidentally, the toe poke is equally effective when you're a defender scrambling to clear a ball out of a dangerous area.

Don't be ashamed to employ the toe-poke. Make it one more tool in your toolbox.

Note for Coaches: The prettiest toe-poke goal I've ever seen is on YouTube. Search *'Ole Miss Goal Taylor.'* I particularly love the announcer's commentary. It was the right surface at the right time to score a critical goal. It's all the evidence you'll ever need to prove that the toe-ball is a worthwhile maneuver.

CHAPTER 23

THE WALL TO NOWHERE

The opponent is awarded a free-kick. The ball is spotted 45 yards out from your goal. What does your team do? It puts together a four-person wall. And the only question left to ask is *Why?* This one is a real head-scratcher and yet it is remarkably common in women's soccer.

The only time you need a wall of more than a single player is when the free-kick is in obvious shooting range. A free-kick from 45 yards away is clearly not shooting range.

Think of it this way: If the ball won't be shot, chances are it will be served. The vast majority of free-kicks inside the attacking half are served into the penalty box as jump balls. The ball will fly into the box and a cluster of bodies will challenge for it. And every person you have in your wall is another person who won't be marking one of the opponents loitering inside your 18. Every player you have committed to your wall is one less player available to challenge for the entry pass or challenge for a knock down or deflection.

Some of the blame for this has to go to goalkeepers because a lot of them are just plain nuts. When the opposition gets a free-kick, goalkeepers build walls like they're professional contractors. Goalkeepers are scared to death of an opponent scoring on a free-kick and they think the best way to prevent that is to build a big, fat wall. But they have to be realistic. They have to be realistic about the shooter's ability and they have to be realistic about their own abilities to stop a shot from 40 yards. And if your goalkeeper is addicted to assembling unnecessary walls, then you need to command your teammates to go against her wishes. If you don't, then some of the blame is on your shoulders, too.

Note for Coaches: It is up to you to design a plan for the assembly of walls. Your team (and especially your goalkeeper) needs to know how many players will be

50

in a wall based on the location of a free-kick. My personal opinion is that if our wall would be more than two steps out past the D, then we don't need a wall. The D is 22 yards in front of the goal. Two steps in front of that is roughly 24 yards from goal. Ten yards past that (where the ball is spotted) is 34 yards. The goalkeeper has got to be expected to save a shot from 34 yards, especially if she gets a clear look at it – which she will if there is no wall to obstruct her view.

CHAPTER 24

THROW-INS

Did you know that even at the college level, throw-ins are basically a coin-flip? College teams only retain possession of their own throw-ins about 50% of the time. Half the time they give it right back to the opponent. It makes you wonder why every coach in the country shouts for possession of the ball when it rolls over the sideline. You may as well let your opponent have it because there's an excellent chance it's coming right back to you.

Here are some tips for keeping possession of your own throw-ins:

When you get the ball in your hands, immediately cock it back behind your head. Too many players hold the ball down in front of their stomachs. Then when they spot their target, they still have to hoist the ball up and back over their heads and then throw it forward. In the second or two it takes to bring the ball up, the opponent has recognized your target and swarmed her. The bottom line is that it just takes too darn long. But when you start with the ball back behind your head, as soon as you spot your target you can zip it into her.

If you throw the ball down the line, don't throw it between your teammate and the sideline as it will assuredly deflect off her and become the opponent's throw-in. This is especially true if you're throwing it to a teammate's head for a flick-on. Her neck is only so long. You can't expect her to crane her neck a foot and a half to get her head to the proper side of the ball. Give the girl a fighting chance.

If your teammate checks back to receive the throw-in, don't bounce it into her. Once the ball bounces, it begins travelling upward and becomes a more difficult ball to handle. Usually it ends up skipping into your target's knees or abdomen and that is a challenging ball to clean up. But if you eliminate the bounce, the ball will be on its way down when it arrives and your teammate can cushion it to the ground or play a one-touch pass or flick-on.

Whenever possible and prudent, play before your opponent is ready. Throw-ins are an excellent chance to catch your opponent napping with her back to the ball. The quicker you execute your throw-in, the more likely your team is to keep the ball.

Note to Coaches: Your team probably takes between 20 and 40 throw-ins per game. Wouldn't it be nice if you could keep more than just half of them? Discuss these strategies with your team. Spend ten minutes of a training session going over them. Trust me, it will make a difference.

CHAPTER 25

DON'T TURN INTO PRESSURE

Note: This chapter does not apply to dribbling 1v1 to take on an opponent who stands in front of you. It's about dribbling to escape pressure and maintain possession of the ball.

The easiest way to give your opponent the ball is to put the ball between her body and yours. So don't. Just don't. There is absolutely no way you can become a decent soccer player if you are habitually turning into pressure.

When you dribble, get your body between the ball and the opponent — *immediately*. And then, for heaven's sake, please don't turn back into her. If you want to cut the ball back, do it to the other side of your body. That will keep your body between the ball and your opponent, allowing you to protect the ball.

During a game your vision is limited because everyone on the field is at eye level. In the heat of a battle with an opponent dogging your every step, it may seem like you have nowhere to go, so you panic, turn back into her and turn over the ball. But if you watch a game that has been videotaped from a high angle, like the top of the bleachers, you begin to see how many options are actually available to you if you just stay calm.

Soccer is a 360° sport. Players aren't obligated to go forward like they are in many other sports. You have a whole 360° worth of options and a single opponent can only account for so many of those degrees. Even if an opponent takes away one entire side, you still have a whole 180° at your disposal. A single opponent can't take away everything. She has to leave you something, so don't panic. Understanding this will give you a much greater sense of composure on the ball, and composure is the foundation of being a smart player.

At Georgia we have a commandment: *It takes more than one of them to take the ball from one of us.* Every player on our roster is expected to have the composure and technical competence to escape pressure and keep the ball from a single opponent. We can't win games if our players lose these individual battles.

In the heat of the moment it may seem inviting to cut the ball back between you and your opponent. *Don't!* Find another way out of it. Trust me, there's always another way. Just stay composed and find it.

This is one of the most fundamental principles of soccer. Learn it and commit to it.

Note for Coaches: 1v1 escaping exercises are excellent ways to improve a player's composure under pressure and her ability to change directions and be deceptive on the dribble. The Escape Tunnel (Diagram 25.1) makes frequent appearances at our training sessions.

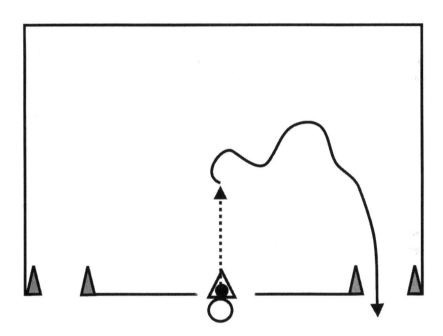

Diagram 25.1 – The Escape Tunnel. The grid is 12 yards wide with a two-yard gate at each end of the start-line, and 8-10 yards long. The attacker starts on the line, feet apart, with the ball between her feet, and the defender directly behind her. The defender pokes the ball through the attacker's legs and play is live. The attacker's objective is to get to the ball first and then dribble her way out of the grid through either of the two gates. The defender wins if she dispossesses the attacker or knocks the ball out of the grid.

CHAPTER 26

THE LAST PLAYER IN POSSESSION NEVER GETS TACKLED. NEVER!

This is a good rule to live by, and it applies mainly (but not exclusively) to defenders.

In the 2006 World Cup game between the U.S. and Ghana, American Claudio Reyna found himself as the last man back and the ball at his feet. Ghana's Haminu Draman nicked the ball off Reyna's foot, danced in alone on goal and tucked his shot neatly inside the far post. Ghana won 2-1.

When you are the closest field-player to your goal and you have the ball at your feet, you absolutely cannot have that ball taken off your foot by the opponent. It is one of the sacred commandments of soccer.

When you find yourself in this position, under no circumstances should you try dribbling past the opponent's forward. I don't care how good you are or how bad she may be, it's not worth the risk because if you lose the ball, your team is in big, big trouble. The opponent who dispossessed you will have a straight and unobstructed path to your goal and that's very bad news. You can't give away those opportunities and expect to win games. So don't even consider dribbling past her unless you have absolutely no other option. It's just not worth it.

Sometimes, especially as a center back, you'll find yourself with the ball at your feet and a bit of room in front of you. The nearest opponent is 15 yards away but she's slowly closing. In these moments you have to remember the rule, because that space can disappear faster than you might imagine and when it does you've got big problems.

In this situation, forget about whether or not the forward can tackle you. That's a fine line and your coach doesn't want you walking it. My rule is this: *Don't let that forward get close enough to even threaten the ball.* Leave yourself a three-yard bubble. Play a little earlier than you might want to play, but make sure that ball is off of your foot before that opponent gets within three yards of you.

Remember, defenders are judged first and foremost by the amount of goals their team concedes. If you can contribute to an attack, swell. But that's just gravy. Remember your priorities and let them govern your decisions. I said it a few sentences ago but it's important enough to repeat: Don't let that forward get close enough to *even threaten* the ball.

Note for Coaches: This is one that will most definitely cost you games, so be 100% certain that your players understand it. The biggest problem is that sometimes your players will break this rule and get away with it. Just because it worked, that doesn't make it right. You've got to hammer home the importance of this concept or you will certainly suffer the consequences.

CHAPTER 27

CLEARING THE FIRST WAVE

In Chapter 26 we discussed the last defender having possession of the ball. This chapter applies to any defender who has the ball.

There are times when you are going to try to play the ball up the field. It could be with a pass. It could be a clearance. It could be on the ground or in the air. It doesn't matter because this applies to all of those situations.

Your pass/clearance absolutely must go beyond the opposition's first wave of pressure.

When you play that ball, there is usually going to be an opponent in front of you. She could be a yard in front of you. She could be ten yards in front of you. Again, it doesn't matter. No matter how far away she is from you, the ball you play must make it past her. You absolutely cannot lose the ball to that first player.

Here are three common scenarios when the opponent blocks or intercepts that pass:

1. She takes clean possession of the ball and is now in a 1v1 against you, which is a fantastic situation for attacking players.

2. She gets control of the ball and has an opportunity to play a ball in behind you to a running teammate.

3. The ball deflects off of her and ends up ricocheting behind you. The attacking player almost always wins this race and when she does she's going to have an excellent chance to be dangerous. Even if you win that race, you are now facing your own goal with pressure on your back. Either way it's not good news for your team.

When a defender gives a ball away to the opponent's first wave, her team is almost always caught numbers down so it almost always ends up with the opponent's quick transition to offense. And it is almost always dangerous so you need to avoid it at all costs.

When you are that defender on the ball, leave yourself some room for error. Play your pass an extra yard wide of the opponent. If you want to play over her head, aim an extra yard or two higher. It's one thing to lose the ball; losing it to that first opponent is another matter entirely. It's just plain unacceptable.

Tip for Coaches: Repeating the advice in Chapter 26, this is another one that will most definitely cost you games so be 100% certain that your players understand it. Blocked clearances often turn into game-changing moments. You've got to make sure your defenders aren't playing for the opponent.

CHAPTER 28

QUICK RESTARTS

The referee whistled for a free-kick 25 yards from goal. The defending team assembled its wall. Its goalkeeper stood hugging her post, shouting directions to properly align the wall. One member of the attacking team was smart enough to realize that the goalkeeper was out of position and paying no attention to the ball. So she quickly stepped up and shot the ball into the empty goal.

If you think that the goalkeeper's mishap was a silly mistake, you're right. If you think that great players don't make silly mistakes, well that's where you're wrong. That goal was scored in the third overtime of an NCAA National Championship final. In the most important game of the year, a national championship was won because one player realized that she could take advantage of a napping opponent.

Even at high levels of soccer, when the referee's whistle blows, a lot of players completely lose their concentration. Every game presents invitations for players to take mental breaks. And smart players are always on the lookout for those moments when they can take advantage of a player who momentarily switches off. Games can be won on quick restarts. And players who are cunning enough to spot those moments can be heroes.

Here's an example from a college team I was coaching. The opposing goalkeeper was whistled for picking up a back-pass and we were awarded an indirect free-kick. The goalkeeper stood at the penalty spot, arms out and palms up, expressing her disbelief to the referee. In one of those palms was the ball. One of my players snatched it from her hand, quickly put it on the ground and passed it to a teammate who shot it into the unguarded goal.

Sounds silly, right? Yep. But that doesn't make it any less factual. Mental breakdowns like that are silly mistakes. But here's the thing... silly happens. And not just to goalkeepers. Silly can happen to everyone.

In an average soccer game, when you include throw-ins, there are upwards of 60 restarts. And if you're paying attention and prepared to play quickly, you can take advantage of many of them. You won't often hit the lottery like the attacking teams in the examples above, but if you're paying attention, once in a while you will. More often than not a successful quick restart will be the beginning of an attack, not the glorious end of one. It can be a throw-in over the defender who has her back to the play. It can be a short free-kick in the middle third that eliminates an opponent who is arguing the call. Whatever the case, when the whistle blows, players switch off. It is not your job to wait for them to switch back on. It is your job to punish them for the mental mistake.

Smart players are always looking for an edge – any edge – that might give their teams a better chance at winning the game. They have the pathology of a pickpocket, always on the lookout for crimes of opportunity. And restarts are an invitation for those crimes.

Obviously there is a very important other side to this coin, and that is when it is the opponent who is awarded the ball for a restart. Smart players are smart enough to assume that the opponent has some pickpockets of its own, so when the whistle blows, not only will the smart player stay switched on, she will also demand that her teammates do the same. I mean, can you imagine being the goalkeeper who handed my team the ball? Can you imagine how embarrassed she was? She switched off for a single second and it cost her team the game. Don't ever let that be you. And don't let it be one of your teammates either.

Your job is not done when the whistle blows. Neither is your opponent's. Use quick restarts to your advantage and prevent your opponent from doing the same.

Note for Coaches: Explain to your team the value and danger of quick restarts. One of the ways we emphasize this is during small-sided (5v5+K) games. We make sure the sidelines are lined with extra balls so when one ball goes out of bounds, there's another one that can be quickly put back into play.

CHAPTER 29

JUDGE HEADERS FOR YOURSELF

Have you ever changed your answer when the teacher asked a question because the person next to you answered differently? Then it turns out that you should have stuck to your guns because your answer was actually the correct one? Yeah, we've all been there. We weren't confident in our own choice so we went with someone else's and ended up paying for it.

As a defender or midfielder, one of your jobs is going to be challenging punts from your opponent's goalkeeper. I cannot count how many times I've seen the attacking player run toward the punt with the defender following tight on her back, only to see the ball fly over top of both of them.

I understand what the defender is thinking. She doesn't want the opponent to get a free header. She wants to be there to put in a challenge. The problem is that a lot of players simply cannot judge punts. And if coaching has taught me one thing, it's that forwards often have no idea where that ball is going to come down.

I've seen examples like the one above where, had the defender simply stood still instead of chasing the forward, the ball would have landed on her head.

Judging flighted balls is part of becoming a good soccer player. If you're not good at it, then you need to get good. Hopefully you have a coach who can help you with that. But once you are competent at judging these punts, have some faith in yourself. Don't let an opponent talk you out of where you think you should be. Let's face it, she may be an idiot.

Note for Coaches: Amazingly enough, I've coached players with youth national team credentials who make this mistake, so don't presume your own players are immune. I haven't figured out a better way to teach this than to simply explain it to my players. Then, if we catch an example on video (and every once in a while we will), I make sure to point it out. The key is teaching your players how to judge a ball for themselves. If they have confidence in that, they are less likely to be swayed by a forward.

CHAPTER 30

READ HER EYES

Let's say there's an opponent on the ball and it's obvious that her next move is to pass the ball. The only thing you don't know is which teammate she intends to pass it to. But many times you can figure it out pretty quickly if you know where to look.

I would say that the vast majority of college soccer players telegraph their passes. Some make it painfully obvious where they intend to pass the ball by their exaggerated approach, the way they stare down their target, and how they shape their bodies. But many others will give you a read if you know where to look.

Almost every player looks at the ball as they are about to strike it. It's where that player looks just before her head goes down that is the key. Most players will take their last look at the place where they intend to pass the ball. And if you watch their eyes and make the physical adjustment, you'll often find yourself in the right place at the right time to intercept that pass.

Some goalkeepers, when faced with a penalty kick, will also employ this tactic. They'll watch the shooter's eyes, and the last place the shooter looks before approaching the ball is the direction that the goalkeeper will guess.

Most players reach the college level with no knowledge of this fundamental concept. And the ones that have it mastered end up looking like savants. After one match an opposing coach was complimenting my center back, pointing out how well she read the game because of the number of passes she intercepted. Sure, it looked like she could *read the game*, but in actuality she was just reading the eyes of the opposing players.

I love the expression 'Reads the game well.' It's as if some players just have a feel for the game, a God-given gift that other players can never develop. Okay, there may be some truth to that, but here's the thing – any player who reads the game well can also read the body language of the ball carrier, and that includes her eyes. And that doesn't happen by accident.

Smart players are habitually spying on the ball carrier's eyes, looking for a half-step head start. That's why they always seem to be in the right place at the right time. Smart players aren't psychic. They just know where to look.

And while we're at it, let's flip this nugget around, because there are going to be times when you are the player on the ball and the opponent will be trying to read your eyes and get a jump on your passes.

One of the most noticeable separating factors between very good players and great players is that great players disguise their passes. Heck, they disguise everything. They disguise where they'll take their first touch. They disguise the direction they will turn the ball. They'll set up to head a ball and then bring it down on their chest. Great players are deception machines.

To climb to that next level, the one thing you cannot do is give the ball away, especially when you are unpressured. We refer to that as giving the ball away cheaply. And clever opponents will be trying to get a read on you by watching your eyes. So you've got to learn to disguise your passes. Master the no-look pass. If your pass is going to your right, make sure your last look is to your left. Play passes with the outside of your foot whenever prudent; you won't have to change your body shape and that will help to disguise your intentions.

Note for Coaches: The defending aspect of this chapter is another concept I haven't figured out how best to teach, but I'm very open to suggestions at www.soccerpoet.com. Teaching players to disguise passes is a little easier and I'll do it with individual or small group sessions where players get a lot of unpressured technical repetitions executing no-look passes.

CHAPTER 31

THE PRE-FAKE

This is a simple skill, but if you don't add it to your game, you will plateau pretty quickly. Everyone knows the importance of being able to use deception when you have possession of the ball. The pre-fake is applying deception before the ball actually arrives at your feet.

Here's a common example: The center back plays a square pass to the left back and the opponent's center forward gives chase. The left back hopes to turn the ball to the outside of her body and play her next pass up the sideline. The question is whether or not she will be able to execute this maneuver before the forward can arrive to destroy the play.

Well, one way the left back can buy herself an extra half-second is to pre-fake by throwing a little hitch move as if she is going to return the ball to the center back with a one-touch pass. That move can (and often will) cause the chasing forward to hesitate. And the extra half-second that pre-fake bought the defender may be the difference between that play succeeding and failing.

As mentioned in the previous chapter, smart players are rich with deceptive talents. They are always leading the opponent in one direction and then going the opposite way. Pre-fakes are a big part of that.

Are you comfortable turning with the outside of your foot? If you are, then try misleading your opponent with a small shoulder fake before you receive the ball. Everything you do is more effective when you add deception.

There's a widely held belief amongst soccer coaches that generally speaking, fast players aren't smart players; that as they move through the ranks of youth soccer, fast players solve their soccer problems with speed and therefore aren't challenged to improve their technical ability. Especially at the younger age groups, the gift of speed robs them of the necessity to develop other critical aspects in their game. Slower players – the ones who aren't guaranteed to

66

win the foot races – depend on technique and deception to solve their soccer problems. That's one reason slower players are often more technically gifted and deceptive as they graduate into the older age groups.

Deception is a prerequisite in soccer. Every player needs to have the ability to escape 1v1 pressure. Not every player needs to be a 1v1 artist who can dribble past an opponent, but every player needs to have the ability to use deception to buy time and space and to shake off an opponent. The pre-fake is a simple tool to add to your game. If you don't have it, get it.

Note for Coaches: We train this concept several different ways. Sometimes it will be in a static passing exercise between partners 20 yards apart so the players get the hang of it technically. If I'm working with the Back 4 on switching fields, I may require each player to execute a pre-fake before receiving the ball and passing it to the next player down the line. And occasionally we'll make the pre-fake a requirement in a possession game. If a player receives a pass without executing a pre-fake, her team forfeits possession. It will make a mess of the exercise for a while, but it will force your players to improve.

CHAPTER 32

THE (NON) DANGEROUS PLAY

We've all experienced this: An opponent falls on the ball. You hover over her waiting for the referee to whistle a dangerous play. Instead, the opponent stands up and maintains possession of the ball and the whistle never blows.

Yes, it can be maddening, but a lot of officials don't want to stop the play until it becomes legitimately dangerous. So you have to make it that way.

Disclaimer: The rest of this chapter in no way, shape or form suggests, recommends or otherwise means to imply that you should intentionally inflict pain or injury on your opponent. As a matter of fact, the whole purpose of this concept is to get the referee to blow the whistle *without* harming your opponent.

Okay, back to our story. How do we get the referee to blow that whistle? By convincing him that the player on the ground is in imminent danger. And how do you do that? Simple.

As soon as that opponent lands on the ball, immediately deliver a rapid succession of toe pokes at the ball. There's no need to wind up and kick – so don't! Just shuffle your feet as close as possible to your fallen opponent's body and poke, poke, poke. Remember, the object is to present an illusion of danger, not actually induce it. If the ball is underneath your opponent you should be able to get your foot underneath her without your toe ever actually touching her.

Okay, so the girl on the ground may get a bit peeved by your aggression and the opposing fans will go mental for about ten seconds, especially when the referee awards the free-kick to you - which he will — but the bottom line is that your team will be given the ball.

Note for Coaches: I don't know of any great way to train this concept. Just show it to your players and hopefully they'll remember it when the time comes.

CHAPTER 33

DEFENDING THE PENALTY KICK

I was coaching a second-year program at a small NAIA school and we were hosting a game against Louisiana State University (LSU) from the SEC. Naturally, we were a massive underdog. But wouldn't you know, we played our tails off that day and to everyone's surprise, with 9 minutes remaining in regulation, the score was tied 0-0. We were on the verge of pulling off one of the biggest upsets in the history of college soccer. And then the unthinkable happened – LSU was awarded a penalty kick.

The referee's whistle had burst our optimistic bubble. The body language of my players was unmistakable. The dream was about to die. It was devastating.

LSU's player stepped up to take the penalty and smashed a shot that would rip the twine to our goalkeeper's right. But we had a darn good goalkeeper and she had guessed correctly. Lunging to full extension she got a hand to the shot and kept it out of the net. But the rebound fell back in front of the goal.

On the video of that play, as our goalkeeper makes the save, you can see three of her teammates literally jumping in celebration as if they themselves had scored. The problem was that no one from our team actually bothered to crash the goal in case of a rebound. An LSU attacker was first to the ball and scored a sitter from six yards.

When your team concedes a penalty kick, the first thing you have to do is assume your goalkeeper will make the save. And if she does make a save, make sure it's the only one she has to make! You can't ask your goalkeeper to make two saves on the same penalty! Our goalkeeper's great save meant nothing because none of her teammates bothered hunting for rebounds.

When a penalty is called, the next five seconds are critical. Most players will switch off. The attacking team will celebrate its good fortune. The defending team will pity its bad luck. You've got to stay switched on and take advantage of this five-second window to do the best you can with the cards you've been dealt. As soon as you hear that whistle, go into damage control, and that means taking up the best positions for rebounds. Immediately claim the prime real estate – the spots where the D intersects the 18 – and don't let anyone push you off of them. Players in these two spots will have the shortest path to any rebounds left lying in front of the goal. Once you've claimed the prime positions, assume there will be a rebound and sprint toward the goal as the ball is leaving the shooter's foot.

Most penalty kicks are going to end up in the goal, but some aren't. You need to take advantage of those times when good fortune smiles down upon you. Smart players give themselves every opportunity to succeed, even against very long odds. They assume a rebound will appear and they position themselves to have the best chance of being first to it. So should you. If you're wrong, you're wrong. So what? But if you're right, you have the chance to be a hero.

Note for Coaches: At UGA we had the exact same situation occur in a 2010 preseason match. Our goalkeeper made the save while her teammates didn't put much thought or effort into hunting the rebound, which the opponent easily finished. We addressed the 'one save' concept immediately after the match. The next day at training we reviewed our positioning on defensive penalties and rehearsed it a few times against live penalties. We were whistled for three more penalties that season and didn't concede a goal on any of them, which only goes to prove that penalty kicks are not automatic and hunting rebounds is worth your time.

CHAPTER 34

COMMON SENSE DEFENDING

How good is your weak foot? Answer honestly. Because if your left foot is as capable as your right foot, then you are a proud member of soccer's tiny minority. Almost every player feels much more comfortable with her strong foot. Very few players are equally adept at striking a ball with either foot.

Knowing that the opponent you are facing is likely going to favor one foot, your first job is to figure out which foot that is. Your next job is to *make her play with the other one.* I cannot possibly overstate how much easier this will make your life.

I want my defenders to figure out the strong foot of the opposing forward within the first five minutes of a match, preferably sooner. The same goes for center midfielders. And if a right-footed player has the ball and plans to play forward, we want to make her do that with her left. If she wants to shoot, we want her shooting with her left. A staggering amount of players won't even take the shot unless the ball is on their strong side.

I arrived at college as a forward and was promptly converted into an outside back which completely freaked me out because I had never played one minute of soccer as a defender. Before our first game our coach told me to keep my opponent on his weak foot, so I did. And it worked – better than I ever imagined. It worked so well that I remember thinking, *Is this all there is to it?* It worked the next game, too; and the game after that and the game after that. As a matter of fact, it never stopped working. It worked so well that it instantly became my first priority when a match began – identify the stronger foot and take it away. I realized that when you take away their dominant foot, a lot of players are completely lost. I felt like I had stumbled onto a pot of gold. The easiest way to defend an opponent was to keep him on his weak foot. *Why hadn't anyone told me this before?*

It's amazing how many players are practically paralyzed when you take away their strong foot. They will try anything to get the ball to their better side. If you can take away the strong foot, you can completely neutralize a lot of players. And that's a good thing. If she's going to beat you, make her do it with her weak foot.

Note for Coaches: This is an easy one that's too good not to implement. Get your players in the habit of identifying an opponent's weak foot and taking away her strong one.

CHAPTER 35

MY BALL, YOUR BALL, THEIR BALL

I bought my first house in 2001. It was basically a glorified surf shack about a block from the beach, but it was a good size and I was thrilled to finally have a place of my own. The living room was very spacious with a beautiful, dark, hardwood floor. That beautiful floor desperately cried out for an area rug, so I set out to find one. The problem was that when it came to matters of decorating, I had no taste whatsoever and had no idea what a good area rug would look like if it walked up and knocked on my door. I don't know how many dozens of area rugs I considered, but it was far more than I ever intended. I'd look at one, think, *This is nice*, and consider buying it. Then I'd look at the next one and think that maybe it was even nicer. Then a few minutes later I'd find one I liked even more. Or maybe not quite as much. I could never be sure. This went on and on and on – from rug to rug, store to store. I liked a lot of those rugs, but I always balked at buying one because I lacked confidence in my taste as an interior decorator and I was afraid that I would soon find a rug that was better than the one I had just bought. I didn't want to end up buying the second-best rug. So instead my floor stayed bare for the next five years.

How can this possibly relate to soccer?

I'm glad you asked.

There's a ball that's travelling directly between you and your teammate. Either one of you could easily handle it, so you decide to make a move for it. Then you start to reconsider your decision. Yes, you could do something with that ball, but your teammate might be in position to do something even better. So you defer to her. The problem is that she just went through the exact same thought process and has deferred to you. Neither of you wanted to do the second-best thing and neither of you took responsibility for communicating; and through your indecisiveness and lack of communication, both of you did nothing. The opponent now has the ball and you're left with a bare floor.

The second-best thing will always be better than the third-best thing. There's a value to being decisive, and the earlier the better. Even if your decision may be the second-best option for your team, it's still better than the option where your team doesn't have the ball anymore. Don't be afraid to be authoritative. Don't make a habit of passing that responsibility onto your teammates. You're better off making a decision that is merely good enough and communicating your intentions loudly and clearly to your teammates as quickly as possible.

Note for Coaches: You'll commonly see this problem when a midfielder, with some pressure tailing her, is chasing a ball back towards one of her own defenders. The midfielder's only option is to dribble laterally to escape while the defender will have a chance to play a forward ball. The two players will often collide or the defender will blast the ball into her teammate. Obviously neither of these are very good options. It's a good idea to have a rule in place that in these situations, the player facing forward has the right of way.

CHAPTER 36

TURNING THE CORNER

This chapter is about a single touch – one simple yet critical touch that will often determine whether or not your team generates a scoring chance.

I'm referring to a player in a wide position, typically a winger in a 4-3-3, who has the ball and has gotten one step behind the outside back. Her next touch decides everything. And in that critical moment, too many players just plain blow it.

If the attacker's next touch is angled at the goal, the attacker gets between the defender and the goal, effectively eliminating the defender. The angled touch forces the defender to make a very difficult choice: surrender or foul. However, if that touch is straight ahead, the attacker won't seal off the defender and the defender has an angle to recover. The amount of players who will take that touch straight ahead is astonishing.

When you have the chance to turn the corner, take it! It may take some daring and courage, but surely you can manage because it is so well worth the risk. For starters, you may be able to stroll right into the six-yard box and score. I've seen it happen. If you're inside the 18 when you turn the corner, you may draw a penalty kick. I've seen that happen, too. But even if that isn't the case, turning the corner will cause the defense all types of problems. If nothing else you will almost assuredly be able to serve an unpressured cross. And that's just the beginning. The real joy comes from how that one touch can completely undo an entire defense.

When you turn the corner, you either eliminate that outside back or you force her to foul you. If she fouls you, you gain a free-kick from a useful position and there's an excellent chance that the foul warrants a yellow card. But if she doesn't foul you and you eliminate her cleanly, that's where the real fun begins because in effect, the defense has lost a player. That means the other defenders must adjust to accommodate their new numerical problem. If the second/supporting defender is marking a player, she must abandon her mark to confront you. In turn, the third defender will have to abandon her mark to pick up the player abandoned by the second defender. The fourth defender will likely have to do the same to pick up the player abandoned by the third defender. All of that switching is incredibly challenging for the defense and can lead to dangerous gaps and unmarked attackers. All because you angled your touch toward the goal.

There is no single, critical touch that is so readily available in our sport. And too many times the winger fails to seal off that outside back and heads straight down to the endline where she launches a blind cross that is hopeful at best. Often times she can't even manage that because the defender has recovered well enough to block the cross.

Let me make my point another way. The defender could not possibly be more thankful if you don't take the opportunity to turn the corner because now she gets a second crack at you. If you don't seal her off, you are doing her an enormous favor.

You cannot be afraid to take that daring, angled touch toward the goal. You cannot be afraid to get fouled in that situation. You may have that chance once in a game, and when you do, you have got to make it count.

And just to hammer home the point... When I'm out recruiting and I see a winger take that aggressive angled touch to seal off the defender and drive at the goal, I perk right up. So few players have the nerve to turn the corner that when I find one who does, I give her my full attention.

Note for Coaches — Often times it is a lack of nerve, not knowledge, which prevents your winger from taking the angled touch because she knows she's putting the defender in a position to foul her. You've got to convince her to take it anyway. Diagram 36.1 is an excellent exercise for training this concept.

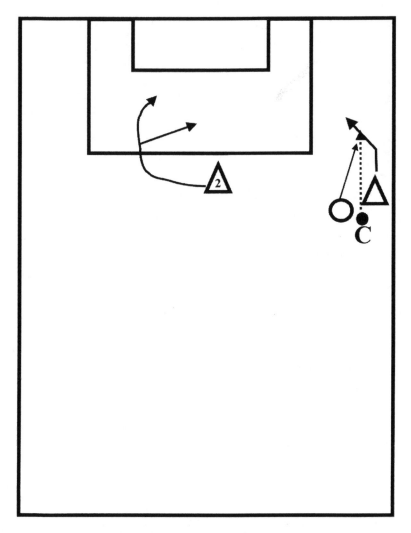

Diagram 36.1 – Turning the Corner. The attacker starts in the wide position and gets a one-yard head start on the defender. The Coach passes a ball between the two of them. The attacker's job is to take a violent touch across the defender to cut her out of the play and then serve a ball to Attacker #2 arriving at the back post or the penalty spot.

CHAPTER 37

FIX YOUR RADAR

In the previous chapter we discussed getting behind a defender then turning the corner and driving at the goal. But you don't always have to be behind the defense before angling your dribble at the center of the goal.

There are times when a player, usually a wide midfielder or an outside back, will have the ball and a lot of space in front of her. The next player with a chance to confront her will be one of the opponent's back four. Too often the ball-carrier will dribble straight down the sideline because that is the path of least resistance. Unfortunately, it's also the least problematic path to defend. Eventually the outside back or center back will step up to confront you and funnel you toward the sideline, allowing the other three defenders to easily maintain their shape to protect the goal. All four defenders will be able to keep the ball and your teammates in their fields of vision. It's Defending 101. To beat a strong defense, you've got to bring a lot more to the table than that.

However, when you run at the heart of the defense, things get a lot trickier for the opponent.

Remember, you give a defense the most problems when you force the defenders to communicate and make decisions. By angling your dribble straight at the goal, you immediately force a decision between the outside back and the center back as to which player will confront the ball carrier. That is the easiest decision they have to make and there's a 50-50 chance they'll get it wrong. Typically they'll hesitate in making the decision and both players will either step up or they'll both retreat. Either way they've got problems.

From there it only gets more difficult.

Even if the defense is organized enough to quickly determine that it should be the center back confronting the dribbler, interior seams open between her and her teammates. Those other defenders must figure out how to close those seams while keeping track of any runners making slashing runs in advance of the ball. Committing the center back is like forcing your opponent to move her king in a chess match – every other piece has to start making adjustments. Now you're forcing defenders to make decisions and communicate. And the slightest failure could result in an unguarded seam that leaves the defense susceptible to being split right up the gut. Additionally, as you run at the heart of the defense, the outside backs must pinch in to protect their goal. This leaves a lot of space out on the wings for your teammates to attack.

This concept sounds more complex than it actually is. Diagram 37.1 will help clarify my point. Or you can just trust me and remember this piece of advice: When you have a gaping space in front of the back four, angle your dribble straight at the heart of the goal. Good things will happen.

Note for Coaches: An excellent exercise to introduce this topic is 3v2+Ks. Mark out a field 40x30 yards with goals on the end-lines. At one goal a defender starts on each post. The three attackers are stretched across the other endline, with the wide attackers starting on the corners. The defenders serve a ball to the attackers and play is live.

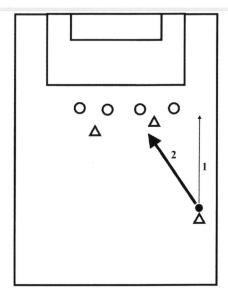

Diagram 37.1 – If the player on the ball chooses Option #1, a straight run down the line, the attack will be very predictable and the opponent will have an easy time maintaining its defensive shape. If the attacker chooses Option #2 and runs straight at the heart of the defense, the defenders have to contest a potential shot while clogging interior seams and tracking forward runners. This forces defenders to communicate and make decisions.

CHAPTER 38

DRAWING PENALTIES

There's an interesting disconnect between men's soccer and women's soccer. In the men's game an attacker will dribble into the opponent's goal area and dive like an Olympian off the high board when a defender sticks a leg out, even if there's been no contact.

Women tend to go to the other extreme, which is equally bad (just not equally reprehensible). Even when enough contact has been made to justify a penalty kick, most female players will fight like crazy to keep their feet and plow ahead. And that lets the referee off the hook.

Technically speaking, you don't have to fall to be awarded a penalty kick. But in the real world the referee isn't going to call it unless you do. Referees don't like to call penalty kicks in the first place. When you stay on your feet it gives the referee an easy way out of doing the difficult part of his job.

When you get fouled inside the 18, don't be a hero – just fall down like your body wants you to do anyway. Why fight it? Chances are that the time spent recovering your balance will negate the scoring chance you once had. If you get fouled in the opponent's goal box, just fall the heck down and take your PK.

Note for Coaches: I would never teach my players to invent contact where there was none and you shouldn't either. On the other hand, you're not running a charity either. Your team should get every PK it legitimately has coming to it. This chapter is a worthwhile discussion to have with your attacking players. The day will come when it wins you a game.

CHAPTER 39

KEEP THE BALL ALIVE

I believe that addressing and training this concept was a major turning point for us during the 2010 season at Georgia. It made such a profound impact that I plan on addressing it with every team I ever coach.

Territorially we were dominant in nearly every game, but we habitually failed to produce the finishing we needed to win. In the attacking third we lacked patience and we lacked discipline. We would press the opponent for long stretches at a time and everything would be going swimmingly. We'd work down the left side, turn around, switch fields and then try the right side, methodically probing for a worthwhile opening. On the sidelines we could see our opponent wilting from the amount of chasing it was forced to do. We could see the opposing players growing tired in body and spirit. We could see that their shape was coming undone and we knew a good scoring chance was just moments away. Then, inevitably, one of our players would lose her patience and hit a low-percentage, off-balance shot from 30 yards that would result in an easy save or a goal kick and would destroy all the momentum we had been building. Or we would attempt a shot from an impossible angle that would sail wide of the post. In effect, we were donating the ball to our opponent for no other reason than someone decided we had gone too long without shooting. It was a very frustrating stretch for us because we were settling for 0-0 ties against teams that we were categorically destroying in the run of play.

Smart players are realistic. They don't let the opponent off the hook with attempts at goal that will never be dangerous. How many goals have you scored from 35 yards? How many have you scored from 35 yards with your weak foot? How many have you scored from 35 yards with your weak foot when you were off balance? If you don't make a habit of scoring from 35 yards... if you haven't done so in three years... maybe you should consider eliminating that choice from your menu.

You need to understand the damage you do to your team when you take unrealistic shots. You need to understand how it affects the big picture. You can't expect to win if you're continually donating the ball to your opponent when you have her on the ropes. Once you understand that, you will become more discerning in your shot selection.

Another common violation of this rule can be found in unrealistic headers, particularly from crosses. When a serve arrives in your opponent's goal area, it arrives as nothing more than the massive potential to become a goal. Your decision upon receiving that cross determines whether or not that potential will be realized.

Too often a player, who has no realistic chance of putting sufficient power on her header, will disregard the odds and try to score anyway. Her shot is an easy grab for the goalkeeper and kills her team's chance to create a legitimate chance.

When you arrive at the back post and that cross has you backpedaling away from the goal, you won't score. If the cross doesn't have much pace and you are 16 yards away from the goal, you won't score. And as much as you scoring a goal would make me very happy, there's a time and a place to go to Plan B. If you don't have a realistic chance to score, don't bother shooting. Don't ruin it for everyone. You're better off keeping the ball alive so a teammate might get that realistic chance. Instead of lobbing a soft header at the goalkeeper or trying to score from an impossible angle, knock the ball down to a teammate or to the top of the six or toward the penalty spot where it can be dangerous.

It's not just headers; it's everything. Regardless of your surface choice, if you're going to take a crack at goal, make sure you have a realistic chance of scoring. It doesn't have to be a no-brainer, automatic easy goal. But by the same token, you shouldn't take a shot that cannot possibly score without the help of divine intervention. Be realistic, patient and disciplined. Otherwise you're donating the ball to your opponent and letting her off the hook.

Note for Coaches: When we addressed this at Georgia, something remarkable happened. Our per-game shot total went down, but our goals-per-shot percentage improved dramatically. Instead of taking 27 shots and not scoring, we were taking 17 shots and scoring three times. We kept the ball in the field of play more, and kept possession of it, which wore down our opponents. Our opponents were taking fewer goal kicks so they weren't getting as much rest. Their goalkeepers were handling the ball less which also took away opportunities to rest. If your team is dominating games but not getting results, this is a topic you may want to evaluate.

CHAPTER 40

THROW-INS AREN'T
AS GREAT AS YOU THINK THEY ARE

If you have the choice to play the ball with your feet under minimal pressure or let it roll out of bounds for a throw-in, play with your feet.

Throw-ins reduce your options and are limited to the distance a player can legally heave the ball. They give the opponent the chance to get numbers near the ball. Most importantly, fifty percent of throw-ins result in a loss of possession. Look at it this way: a throw-in is a 50-50 ball. Trying to keep possession from a throw-in in your own defensive third is like trying to organize a jailbreak in broad daylight. It's not impossible, but there's a really good chance you're going to get shot.

There are certainly times to let the ball roll over the sideline, like when you are under immediate pressure, or when you are trying to kill the clock to preserve a lead, or in your attacking third if your teammate has a long throw-in that can directly create a goal scoring opportunity. Yes, there are exceptions. But generally speaking, if it doesn't provide you with a distinct advantage, keep the ball in play and use your feet to move the ball. You will have more options and a better chance of helping your team maintain possession of the ball. Besides, almost every player can kick the ball farther than she can throw it; if nothing else, keeping the ball in play allows you to relieve pressure by whacking the ball up the field.

Note for Coaches: I don't know why so many players don't understand this concept. I don't know why they feel that throw-ins are so advantageous. But I know that smart players understand that there is a time to let the ball roll out of bounds and a time to keep it in play.

CHAPTER 41

HUNTING REBOUNDS

Any player I've ever coached will tell you I'm a freak for hunting rebounds. And I have no idea why any player or coach wouldn't share my zeal.

At the highest level of men's soccer, goals are commonly scored from rebounds. As a matter of fact, a rebound provided the most exciting moment of the 2010 World Cup for the United States. Landon Donovan's goal in the 90th minute that defeated Algeria was a very simple rebound finish. Rebounds happen in men's soccer all the time. But they happen even more in the women's game.

Women use the same size goal as the men but the goalkeepers aren't as tall and their arms aren't as long. That means shots that a male keeper can reach and hold, a female keeper might only be able to reach. Males and females also use the same size soccer ball, but the hands of a female goalkeeper are smaller and more prone to coughing up rebounds. In addition to goalkeepers, there's also the matter of goalposts and crossbars. Plenty of shots find their way off the woodwork and back in front of the goal. My point is, rebounds happen. They happen a lot. And a smart player can cash in on them.

The key to hunting rebounds is very simple: *EXPECT THEM.* The reason that most players don't capitalize on rebounds is that they don't go after them until after they appear. They aren't proactive.

When a shot is taken, there is usually at least one defender between the attackers and the goal. When a rebound occurs, that defender will have a head start on the attackers and therefore she will usually be first to the ball. To be an effective hunter of rebounds you have to negate her head start. That requires two things: You have to recognize when a teammate is about to shoot and when you see that, you have to crash the goal. It's that simple. To eliminate the defenders' head start, you've got to hunt rebounds before they actually materialize. You have to crash the goal and *hope* there will be a rebound. That's the whole key to this. The vast majority of attackers aren't proactive in hunting rebounds. They wait until a rebound happens and then they react to it. And that's why they finish second in the race to the ball. Smart forwards know to run as the shot is about to be taken... *just in case.*

In 2011, our team at Georgia was tied 1-1 with a very inspired and hard-working team from Mercer University. Mercer had kicked our tail for the first 45 minutes but we had retaken control after half-time. We outshot the Bears 15-5 in the second half, but we couldn't manage to actually put the ball into the back of the net, so the game went into Golden Goal overtime. It was a nerve-wracking night for us because a loss to Mercer would likely extinguish any chance we had to make the NCAA Tournament. We couldn't afford to lose or tie that game. It was without question, a *must-win.*

Nine minutes into the first overtime, our center forward Ashley Miller, took a shot from 18 yards that was blocked. The ball deflected back to Jamie Pollock who sidestepped a defender then laced a drive at the Mercer goal. The goalkeeper stretched out to make a diving save but the ball trickled along the goal-line where it was tapped in by our left wing, Lex Newfield. Lex's finish was simple, but her work leading up to it was sheer brilliance. It was the quintessential work of a rebound hunter.

Everyone watching the game saw Lex follow up on Pollock's shot. What no one probably noticed was that Lex initially made a run at the goal when Miller was about to shoot. When Miller's shot was blocked, Lex quickly about-faced to sprint back onside and then immediately spun back toward the goal as Pollock prepared to shoot. When Lex got to the ball, there wasn't a defender anywhere near her - all of them had stopped to watch the goalkeeper make the save. Because Lex anticipated that a rebound *might* materialize (Twice!), she got to score the game-winning goal and be a hero in front of 1500 very excited fans. Now isn't that worth running six or seven yards... *just in case?*

In my book *Everything Your Coach Never Told You Because You're A Girl*, I go into great detail about a team that practically made a living hunting rebounds. That team was so notorious for scoring rebounds that as its reputation for second-chance finishes grew, opposing goalkeepers were rattled before the games even kicked off. Those goalkeepers knew that if they didn't hold every single shot that came their way, they were going to get punished. And ironically enough, that panicked mindset actually led to more dropped balls, more rebounds and more goals.

One of the best goalkeepers I've ever coached, a consensus All-American, confirmed my affinity for hunting rebounds. She said that rebounds were cyclical – the more you hunt them the more likely they are to materialize because goalkeepers get unnerved when an opposing forward is bearing down on them. She was right.

Become a fanatical hunter of rebounds. In soccer there is nothing else that offers such great rewards for such a minimal amount of work. Rebounds win games.

Note for Coaches: Hunting rebounds is not about talent. Hunting rebounds is a mentality that gives otherwise average players a chance to make an impact on your results. I like to develop that mentality in my teams through small-sided games where rebound goals are worth two points and all other goals are worth one.

CHAPTER 42

BAIT AND SWITCH

In an earlier chapter we discussed the importance of the last defender not losing the ball. If that concept is important enough to warrant a chapter, then its
reciprocal is also. Let me give you a common example.

Team A hits a big, flighted clearance that will be played by the center-back
on Team B. That center-back will have the option of bringing the ball down or
clearing it with a header or volley. Her decision will be based on the pressure
applied by the opposing forward. Typically that forward goes bombing in, leaving the defender no choice but to clear the ball back up the field. The forward's
hard work is admirable, but it has done her team no practical good. So let me
give you a better option.

If you are the forward in this situation, you have to judge whether or not
you can get to that defender in time to win the ball outright or at least disrupt
her clearance. If you think you can do that, then step on the gas and go for it!
If not, you may be able to set a trap. Instead of plowing toward that defender
and panicking her into a clearance, put on the brakes about seven or eight yards
in front of her and encourage her to settle the ball. Once she has committed to
something other than a first-time clearance, you have a chance to take the ball
from her and get behind the entire defense.

There are two keys to doing this effectively. The first is being a good actor.
You've got to lull that defender into a sense of false confidence. You've got to
make her believe that she will have time on the ball. She has to feel comfortable
bringing that ball down to her feet. Otherwise she's just going to clear it.

The second key is your ability to read the defender's body language. A
moment before the ball actually gets to her, she will disclose her intentions. The
instant you recognize she has decided against a first-time clearance, sprint right
at her with everything you've got because now you do want to panic her! You

want to panic her into a bad first touch. She needs to think that you are going to run right over the top of her! If her first touch is less than stellar, you can capitalize on it.

Will this always work? No. Or at least, not entirely. Sometimes the defender will just clear it anyway. Other times she will still be able to bring the ball down and get rid of it without you making a significant impact. But that's okay. The brilliance of this maneuver is found in the risk-reward ratio because you're never going to end up worse off than you started. Even if you don't directly strip the defender of the ball, more often than not your execution of the bait and switch will provide your team with some type of benefit – something better than that defender's free clearance. You may force her into a bad pass or a poor clearance or some type of slow play that puts her team at risk. Regardless, it won't hurt your team any more than her bombing the ball back up the park. And if you happen to hit the lottery and take the ball off her foot, well then you've got the chance to cause big problems.

Note for Coaches: As with hunting rebounds, this is another concept that gives a forward with limited technical ability the chance to still be very effective. If you can teach your forwards how to recognize and execute the bait and switch, you'll regularly put opponents in compromising positions.

CHAPTER 43

MISMATCHES ON PUNTS, GOAL KICKS and CORNER KICKS

Dear Goalkeepers,

I'll say this as plainly as I possibly can. If your punts kept getting shoved back down your team's throat because one player on the other team is dominating in the air, STOP AIMING AT HER. For heaven's sake, *figure it out and make the adjustment*. One of the best headers on almost any team is the defensive center midfielder and she's normally the one who will be challenging for your punts. If she is single-handedly destroying your team in the air, then stop giving her that opportunity. Just aim somewhere else. Angle your punts to the right. Angle your punts to the left. Start throwing the ball out to your defenders. I really don't care. Just apply some common sense and stop kicking the ball to the opponent who is killing your team. Makes sense, right? The same logic also applies to goal kicks.

Pay attention to the man-to-man match-ups on corner kicks and free-kicks. If you have a scouting report, then you should obviously have your team's best headers matched up against the opponent's best headers. If you don't have a report, just figure it out by height. You don't have to break out a tape measure and be absolutely perfect. Just make sure your 5'4" teammate isn't marking the opponent's 5'11" player. If you see a midget marking a giant, fix it.

Smart goalkeepers pay attention to these things. You should, too.

Note for Coaches: Most goalkeepers judge their punts and goal kicks by how far the ball went and pay little attention to what happens when it comes back to earth. Ask your goalkeeper to pay attention to the end result. She won't. But ask her anyway.

CHAPTER 44

CUT OFF THE RETURN PASS

If you want to drive your coach insane, don't follow the advice I'm about to give you.

When you are chasing a pass from one opponent to another, make sure that you cut off the player who initially passed the ball. If you don't, the player who receives the pass is going to pass the ball straight back to the first player and you're going to end up as the monkey in the middle.

As the ball leaves the opponent's foot, it travels a straight line to her teammate. The path you take to chase the ball should be directly along that line as if the ball were pulling you along by a string. If the original passer doesn't quickly move to change her angle of support, you've cut her out as an option for a return pass. This frees you up to pressure the player who received the initial pass because she has one less option available to her. If you don't chase along that line, the two opponents will be able to pass back and forth all day and you'll be spinning in circles.

Regardless of your position, you're going to have to do some defending. When you are the first defender, try to do at least two jobs: pressure the ball and take away at least one passing option. You can start by taking away the player who made the initial pass.

Note for Coaches: Forwards are the main culprits when it comes to violating this concept. A forward will work really hard to chase a pass from the left back to the center back, but because she doesn't chase at the proper angle, the center back will simply return the ball to the left back. All of the forward's hard work is for naught and the opponent easily breaks pressure.

CHAPTER 45

PLAYING AGAINST A KILLER WIND

On a windy day the first thing you have to decide is how big of a factor is the wind going to be when it's against you. Is it going to make it difficult to attack? Or is it going to make it impossible?

One day I was recruiting in Las Vegas and the winds were absolutely hellacious, blowing directly north-south as the fields ran. It was so windy that anytime a spectator stood up his chair was immediately blown away. It turned the games into a circus. That day I saw three goals from direct free-kicks taken from inside the center circle! I saw a U-15 goalkeeper score on a punt that bounced *twice* and still flew over the opposing goalkeeper's head! One goal kick (taken against the wind) stopped in midair, did an about-face and then scooted back across the endline for a corner kick. It was *that* windy!

Every game that day was divided into two halves: There was the half when you had the wind at your back, and then there was the half where you weren't going to score. Every single goal that day was scored at the same end of the field. EVERY SINGLE ONE!

When faced with a headwind that strong, your first priority is to shorten the half. If you're playing a 90 minute game, the opponent has the wind at her back (and a significant advantage) for 45 minutes. Every minute of time you can bleed off that clock is one less minute your opponent has to score.

Obviously the score of the game may dictate a different approach. For example, if it's the second half and you are losing, then the time-wasting tactic obviously won't do you any good. At that point you just have to play as if that wind was manageable and not impossible. So that's what we'll discuss now.

If you're playing against a strong but manageable headwind, or if you have no choice but to press forward against a howling wind, your decisions mean everything. And the first decision you absolutely must make is to consciously adjust to the situation. You may have to change the way you play. You may have to change the way you've played for every single game of your soccer life. But you can't pretend that it's business as usual. You can't pretend the wind isn't there and that it won't influence the ball. You're going to have to make adjustments. Accept it. That's Step One. Can we agree on this?

The ball is going to get hung up in the air. The higher the ball goes, the more the wind will fight it. So the obvious first adjustment is to try to keep the ball on the ground as much as possible. Even that will be difficult if the wind is blowing strongly enough, but you've got to try. If your passing is good enough you can still play your way up the field beneath the stiffest gusts.

Use common sense when judging flighted balls such as punts, goal kicks, corner kicks and even throw-ins. They are going to end up going deeper than you're accustomed to. Start deeper than you normally would and start deeper than you think you need to. It's a lot easier to make adjustments coming forward than going backwards. Give yourself plenty of margin for error.

Additionally, there are two ways you can actually use a strong wind to your advantage when it is against you. The first way is to pound balls in behind the opponent's line of defenders when the situation allows for it. On a day when the winds are calm, most of these balls will either roll into the goalkeeper or over the endline. But a strong headwind wind will hold those balls up and your forwards will have a chance to run onto them. The key is that your service actually makes it beyond the opponent's back line, and that means you are going to have to kick it harder, maybe a lot harder, than you normally would. Remember, you agreed to change the way you played, right? Well this is the perfect time. Don't expect the ball to travel as far as it normally would. You're going to have to swing your leg harder to make sure the ball clears the line of defenders. Because if even one of those passes gets in behind, it could result in a goal.

The other way to use an opposing wind to your advantage is defensively. Try to follow me here.

I played center field for my high school baseball team. One team we played against had a notoriously short ballpark. The distance from home plate to the center field fence was 310 feet. At most schools, including our own, the distance was closer to 400. I assumed that I would just position myself on the warning track because that was about as deep as I could possibly play. But our coach was clever enough to take a completely opposite approach. He instructed us to play very shallow, about fifteen yards behind the infield dirt. We were going to concede the run-of-the-mill fly balls because they were going to end up over the fence anyway. We couldn't take away home runs so instead we would take away singles. Our job was to prevent line drives from dropping in front of us for base hits. It worked like a charm. We took away a lot of would-be base hits and just as our coach predicted, pretty much any fly ball flew out of the park for a home run anyway. Fifteen years later I adapted this strategy to combat a gale force wind on a soccer field.

Instead of sitting back to defend, we pushed our line of defenders as high as we could and held it there. Our goal was to prevent the opponent from playing underneath us. We took away their ability to play into the feet of their forwards and forced them to play balls over the top of us. On a calmer day it would have been breakaway city, but with the wind pushing the ball with so much force, the opposing forwards were never going to catch up to the through-balls. All of their attempts to play behind us either rolled over the endline or were easily handled by our goalkeeper. The tactic worked beautifully and we won 2-0.

It bears mentioning that when playing into a strong headwind, your goal-keeper needs to be aggressive in coming out of the 18 because she will be able to cut out a lot of your opponent's through-balls.

Note for Coaches: When you're facing any external condition that will play a prevalent role, make sure your players understand the adjustments they have to make BEFORE THE GAME BEGINS. You need to flatten out the learning curve. You don't want 20 minutes of the game to elapse before your players start adapting to the conditions. Before these games I make a point of hammering home the fact that our players must change the way they play, and I insist that they tell me they understand what I'm talking about.

CHAPTER 46

PLAYING WITH A TAILWIND

A strong wind at your back can be a great advantage, *if* you know how to use it. Each team will get that wind for one half, so you've got to do more than just dominate territorially. When that wind is at your back, you absolutely must find a way to put points on the board. If you start with the wind and get to half-time with no goals to show for it, all you've done is hand your opponent a moral victory and an excellent chance to win the game.

Here are some considerations when playing with a strong tailwind:

First of all, you want the ball on the field as much as possible, so recruit some help. In that Las Vegas tournament I mentioned in the previous chapter, it didn't take very long for one team to figure out that its missed shots would end up a couple hundred yards down the complex and allow the opponent to take a minute off the clock every time they were awarded a goal kick. So the parents pitched in to form a human fence behind the opponent's goal to shag the errant shots. Once one team did it, every other team's parents followed suit.

Your forwards have to get the ball at their feet. This is where most teams lose the plot. With a strong wind at their back adding distance to their kicks, most players feel an obligation to play through-balls and balls over the top. But it's a trap! The strong wind will push these balls over the end-line or into the goalkeeper. When you're riding a strong tailwind, you have to take the field one chunk at a time. Once you near midfield, angle your through-balls toward the corners of the 18. Straight balls will end up off the field or in the goalkeeper's hands and precious seconds will tick away. The failure to anticipate how the wind will affect through-balls is how teams waste the advantage a tailwind should provide.

Make sure your corner kicks stay in bounds. The wind can only help you if the ball is in the field of play. If you normally aim for the six, adjust and aim for the penalty spot.

Hunt rebounds! Windy days are exceptionally conducive to producing rebounds because the ball is more likely to knuckle, so crash the goal whenever a teammate winds up to shoot.

Don't force bad shots. Stay realistic. With a strong tailwind, a lot of players start taking unrealistic shots, hoping the wind will turn them into goals. Those shots usually sail over or wide of the goal and more precious seconds tick away. Yes, the wind will provide you with some extra power and will extend your shooting range, but it cannot make up for technical failures. You still have to be balanced and execute good technique.

Note for Coaches: When you have strong wind at your back you may want to take some risks, even in the first half. If the wind will make it very difficult for the opponent to launch an attack, consider making adjustments to your system and personnel. You may want to switch from four defenders to three to allow for an extra attacker. If you have an exceptionally fast defender, consider moving her up top. Remember, you may only have forty-five minutes to win the game.

CHAPTER 47

PLAYING IN THE RAIN

Exactly as we discussed in the previous two chapters dealing with strong winds, when the field gets wet you've got to be prepared to make adjustments to the way you play. When dealing with the wind you can split the game into two halves – the half with a headwind, and the half with a tailwind. But when it rains, the conditions are basically the same for both teams for 90 minutes. The team that makes its adjustments first might stake out a big enough advantage to win the game. Here are a few strategies for dealing with a wet field.

Make sure you have the proper footwear, namely screw-in cleats. When the field gets wet, screw-ins are going to give you the best chance to keep your footing. If you can't change directions without falling down, you're pretty useless as a soccer player. Make the investment and buy a pair of screw-ins. As a matter of fact, buy two pair. Read on to find out why.

Whenever possible, travel with an extra pair of shoes and socks. If you're playing on a wet field, change into your dry gear at half-time. If your footwear is saturated, your legs are lugging around a couple of extra pounds. Why not start the second half lighter and faster than you ended the first? If your team has the capability, change into a whole new dry uniform.

Be aware of the first bounce. On a slick field, a ball that travels through the air like a line drive will pick up speed on the first bounce. Many of these balls will skip past a player who hasn't learned to adjust to the conditions. When that ball is in flight, move your feet to put your body into the path of the ball. Make sure that if you can't control the ball, you at least prevent it from getting behind you. This is an especially important adjustment for your defenders to make or balls will skitter past them and put your team in serious danger.

Reciprocally, on a wet field, a ball that is about to bounce in front of a defender can present a clever forward with a great opportunity to gamble. Typically, as a defender is about to receive an opponent's clearance, the pressuring forward will move to a goal-side position to prevent that defender from advancing the ball on the dribble. But if the ball looks like it will bounce in front of that defender, the forward may want to abandon her defensive responsibility and run in behind the defender, gambling that the ball will skip past the opponent. If the gamble pays off, the forward will be running in alone on goal. The key to this is reading the flight of the ball and the defender's body language as the ball approaches. The forward has to genuinely believe that the ball will make its way past the defender before taking that gamble. If she's not making those considerations, then she's just being lazy about her defensive responsibilities.

Wet fields are also excellent manufacturers of rebounds. The ball is wet and difficult for a goalkeeper to hold, particularly if it skips in at her with pace. It is critically important that attackers put their shots on frame. On a wet field, the first shot will often produce a second shot. But none of that will matter if teammates aren't crashing the goal to hunt for rebounds. Even on a dry field, the key to getting to rebounds is expecting them to appear before the save is ever made. A wet field increases the likelihood of a goalkeeper putting the ball back on the ground.

So far we've talked about a wet field. But some days the field gets enough rain to produce puddles of standing water. For the rest of this chapter we're going to concern ourselves with those fields that have so much standing water that the field is on the brink of being deemed unplayable.

The first key is to accept that you cannot change the conditions, so you're just going to have to change the way you play. You may have to completely abandon your style. That's life. And soccer. Don't bang your head against an unmovable wall. Adjust. If the ground is unplayable, then take the game to the air.

At Georgia we consider ourselves a possession team. We want to keep the ball on the ground and string passes together. We want to make the other team chase. That's how we *want* to play. But life doesn't always work out the way we like.

In 2010 we had a home match against Arkansas. The field was wet in the first half, but with the exception of one big puddle, it was very playable. Late in the first half the skies opened up and we were hit with a continuous torrential downpour. The entire field became standing water. It became literally impossible to pass a ball on the ground more than 5 yards. The ball would simply die in a pool of water. Dribbling was no better. Players trying to advance the ball on the dribble would inevitably overrun the ball that had stopped dead in a puddle. The only way to advance the ball was in the air. At half-time we instructed our players to do just that. No one was to even attempt to dribble at an opponent. Whenever possible our players were to bang the ball forward, *in the air*, with their first touch. We didn't want them trapping a ball unless absolutely necessary. Our objective was to put the ball in the air and aim it at our opponent's penalty spot whenever possible. The key was to get the ball in front of the Arkansas goal. If you can put the ball into dangerous places in those conditions, anything can happen. We weren't going to score a pretty goal in those conditions, so we did our best to score an ugly one.

One particularly effective maneuver was for players who received the ball in a puddle to scoop it out of the water with their first touch, as if they were about to juggle. Once the ball was lifted out of the puddle, the player could smack it down the field with a big volley.

When the field gets overrun with standing water, it's no longer about pretty soccer. It's about territory. Get the ball in the air and down the field and in front of the opponent's goal. When pretty goals aren't on the menu, do your best to score some ugly ones.

Note for Coaches: In pregame warm-up, have your players hit driven and bent balls to one another from 25 yards or greater that will skip into their target on one bounce. Make them aware of how that first bounce will affect the ball and make sure they move their feet to get their bodies into the ball's path.

CHAPTER 48

THE RED CARD CONONDRUM

You've heard of the make-up call. A baseball umpire sees a fastball down the middle and calls it a ball. The next pitch skips off the dirt and is called a strike. A basketball referee regrets a foul he called against one team so he quickly invents a foul against the opposing team to even things out. You see these in every sport at every level, including soccer.

Good referees with intestinal fortitude don't let their last call influence their next one. If your team is fortunate enough to have one of these guys officiating every one of your games, then this chapter won't apply. However, on the off chance that you aren't always blessed with world-class referees turning in a world-class performance, I recommend you read on.

All soccer referees hate making calls that will profoundly impact a game. It positions them as a factor in the result and they aren't looking for that kind of grief. Specifically, referees would rather not award penalty kicks or issue red cards.

You've got to remember that in spite of the insanity it takes to actually want to be a referee, these officials are, at heart, people, too. They want fairness. They don't want to give one team a remarkable advantage and they sure as heck don't want the avalanche of animosity that one of these game-changing calls will surely heap upon them. That's why referees avoid making these calls if at all possible. Most referees have to be practically cornered into whistling a penalty kick or issuing a red card. So if you're on the team that benefits from one of these decisions – *look out!*

Every referee in the world will debate me on this, but I've seen what I've seen too many times. When Team A is awarded a penalty kick, chances are Team B will be awarded one before the game is over. And if Team A is the benefactor of *two* penalty kicks, I'd bet my right arm that Team B will be awarded at least one. The same applies to red cards. Referees do not want to be the deciding factor in a result, so after a game-changing call, they will periodically cave to human nature and look for an opportunity to even things out. That's just the way it is, so you've got to anticipate their humanity and make adjustments.

If the referee has just ejected a player from the opposing team, you've got to watch your step. At that point you should assume a normal foul is a yellow card foul and a yellow card foul is now a red card foul. Once an opponent has been sent off, assume the referee is on the hunt and adjust your game. Don't trip an opponent. Don't argue a call. Just grin and bear it and play the cleanest game you can possibly play. You must not give that referee any excuse to put you in the book. It might not seem particularly fair, but that's how the soccer world spins.

If your team has scored on a penalty kick (especially if that penalty kick has given your team the lead), you have got to play very carefully inside of your own 18-yard box. Some referees have a funny way of finding a reason to negate the advantage they feel they've given your team. And it doesn't have to begin with something as extreme as a penalty kick.

We can draw a stunning example from the 2010 World Cup match between the U.S. and Slovenia when Maurice Edu's goal in the 85th minute was disallowed for a phantom foul. The goal was set up when the referee whistled a foul in favor of the U.S. in the Slovenian defensive third. Landon Donovan served the restart into the Slovenian goalmouth where Edu finished it with a smashing volley. The referee negated the goal by whistling a foul against an unspecified American.

My guess, and I'm hardly alone on this, is that the referee regretted calling the initial foul and had his mind made up to negate the situation by immediately inventing a second foul as soon as the kick was taken, this time against the U.S. Video replay confirms that any fouls worth calling would have been against Slovenia and that the referee was preparing to blow his whistle as Donovan was approaching to take the free-kick. It was the quintessential make-up call and it backfired mightily.

Keep in mind that the World Cup is not only a showcase of the world's best players, but also of the world's best officials. If one of the world's best referees can be a victim of human nature, then don't underestimate the guilt reflex of your own officials.

Smart players recognize these tide-changing events and make adjustments. They are careful not to give the referee an easy reason to even the score.

Note for Coaches: This is another lesson you don't want to learn the hard way. Have this talk with your team so they're prepared when the time comes.

CHAPTER 49

CELEBRATE GOOD TIMES

Chances are you've already been involved in this situation. If you haven't, one day you will.

Someone on your team will take a shot that will hit the underside of the crossbar and deflect almost straight down. The ball will land across the goal-line then bounce straight up - and that's where the chaos will begin. It has been my experience that referees will get this call wrong at least as many times as they get it right. That's why they need your help.

First of all, if you clearly have the chance to get to the ball first and run it into the goal, do it! That takes all the mystery out of the referee's decision. Even if you absolutely know the ball crossed the line, don't take any unnecessary chances. Do your best to make sure the ball physically touches the net. Don't give the referee the chance to take away a goal your team has earned.

If no one on your team has the chance to stuff the ball into the net, the referee's decision will often be based on the reaction of the players involved. A smart goalkeeper will grab that ball, run to the top of the 18 and punt it away as if nothing ever happened. If the referee hasn't ruled it a goal by the time the ball leaves the goalkeeper's foot, he never will. You can't let the goalkeeper's reaction be the only one the referee factors into his decision.

If you know the ball crossed the goal-line, don't look to the referee for confirmation. Don't let your expression say, "Well??? I think it was a goal. What do *you* think?" Don't wait for his answer because there's an excellent chance you won't like it. This is not a call the referee wants to make. He certainly doesn't want to invent a goal for a team that hasn't earned it. It is easier for an official to disallow a legitimate goal than to award one that may not have existed. Make sure the referee knows how you feel about the situation. When the ball crosses that line, immediately (and I do mean *immediately*) celebrate like you just won the World Cup! Your reaction should be larger than life! It should tell him that there is no doubt whatsoever that the ball made it across the line. Convince the referee that there is absolutely no question about what just happened. Make it impossible for him to rule in the opponent's favor. Make him feel like only an idiot would disallow that perfectly good goal. It will win you a game. Someday, somewhere, it most certainly will.

Note for Coaches: This will happen to your team. Coach long enough and believe me, it will happen. The problem is that you just don't know when and where. It is worth two minutes of your time to review this with your players.

CHAPTER 50

CLOCK MANAGEMENT WITH THE LEAD

If there is one glaring tactical difference between men's and women's soccer, this is it. Very few females reach the collegiate level with any concept of clock management and how to kill the game when they have a lead.

The bottom line is that a one-goal lead is good enough to win you the game. When you have that lead and there are ten minutes left and the opponent is throwing everything and the kitchen sink at you in search of the equalizer, above all else, you must not help their cause!

Let me say that there are definitely times when your team will be better served by taking a quick throw-in or free-kick even while hanging onto a slim lead. In some instances a quick restart will actually enable you to kill *more* clock or create the goal that will put the game out of reach. The rest of this chapter will *NOT* be about those times.

Here are some fundamental ways to milk some seconds off the clock:

Don't get cute. If your team is under a lot of heat and you break pressure in the middle third, don't be afraid to whack the ball far up the field, preferably beyond the line of defenders and toward the corners. I've seen so many examples where a player has the chance to force the opponent into retreating deep to retrieve the ball, but instead elects to play a short pass underneath the opponent's back line. That pass gets intercepted and instead of killing the clock and forcing the opponent to expend some energy, the opponent stuffs the ball right back down our throat. Not every job calls for an artist. Ditch-diggers do important jobs, too. When your team is hanging on for dear life, pretty doesn't matter. Winning the game matters – and it is the only thing that matters.

For the love of God don't retrieve the ball for your opponent. Every second she spends retrieving the ball is one less second her team has to produce the tying goal. If the opposing team is awarded a free-kick, make one of its players collect the ball and get it back to the spot of the foul. Even if that ball rolls right up on your foot and balances on top of your shoe, do not kick it back to your opponent. Make her come and get it. This rule also applies to players on the bench, because they screw it up as much as anyone. If the ball is about to bounce across the sideline, get the heck out of the way! Remember whose team you're on!

Don't campaign for yellow cards. This is another one I see every year and it baffles me. Team A is desperately clinging to a one-goal lead with two minutes left in the match. Team B is all over them but a player from Team A has the chance to break pressure. A player from Team B commits a foul to prevent the counter attack. It's a hard foul and probably warrants a yellow card - which is exactly what everyone from Team A (including the coach) starts screaming for. The referee feels backed into the call and stops the clock to issue a yellow card.

In that situation the last thing in the world you want the referee to do is stop the clock. You can run a solid 30-40 seconds off the scoreboard setting up that free-kick. Instead the referee stops the clock and the offending player gets a slap on the wrist.

What good will that yellow card do you (unless it is the offending player's second bookable offense)? It might momentarily give you a sense of cosmic justice, but that's about it. There are two minutes left! Don't cut off your nose to spite your face! Think big picture. What do you gain from that yellow card? What's the chance of that same player picking up another yellow card in those final two minutes? Trust me here. You are better off just letting the clock run and letting the opponent get away with one. Your frustration will pass when the game ends and you've won.

And while we're on the topic, by all means *don't take a yellow card yourself!* In 2009 our team at Ole Miss was clinging to a 1-0 lead against Memphis. We were whistled for a foul 25 yards straight out from our goal with 10 seconds left in regulation. One of our players didn't want to let Memphis take the kick quickly, so she stood in front of the ball – which is fine if you also back away from it in a timely manner, which our player did not do. The crowd was so loud that our player couldn't hear us yelling at her, screaming at her, begging her to back away from the ball. The referee stopped the clock with two seconds remaining to issue her a yellow card. So instead of Memphis having to scramble to get a shot off amidst the chaos of an expiring clock, now they had the luxury of getting the player they wanted on the ball and putting ten of her teammates in front of our goal. Thankfully the shot sailed over the crossbar and we got the win, but we sure did our best to help them tie the score.

Don't run to take a throw-in or corner kick. Why? Because that's just plain dumb. As a matter of fact, if you are the closest player to the ball when it goes out of bounds, you shouldn't be the one throwing it in or taking the corner. When that ball crosses over the line, just walk away from it. Walk toward the center of the field. Walk away from that ball like it's carrying a disease. Let one of your teammates who is farther away make the long voyage to the sideline. It will take her longer to put the ball back in play and thus more time will run off the clock.

Retrieve the ball yourself. At the college level we have ball-shaggers all around the field. Nothing keeps time on the clock more effectively than a hard working ball-shagger. As soon as one ball goes out, they make another one available pretty quickly. When you have the lead, industrious ball-shaggers are your enemy. But occasionally you will have the opportunity to take them out of the equation. Whenever possible, instead of letting the ball-shagger toss you a ball, casually jog to retrieve the ball that went out of bounds. It will allow you to work some more time off the clock. This is especially true for goalkeepers when a shot flies past your goal. Don't stand there asking for a replacement ball, because you'll have that in a matter of three of four seconds. Instead, go chase the ball that went out of bounds. You may have to pretend that you don't see the ball-kid standing there, but more often than not you'll get away with it. This is one of the most effective ways to dispose of big chunks of time.

Kick the ball over the fence. If you are going to kick the ball out of bounds anyway, make it difficult for the opponent to restart it quickly. If there is a fence around your field, kick the ball over it. If the field is surrounded by woods, hoof the ball deep into the woods. Even if a ball-shagger can supply a replacement ball, she still has to go and retrieve the ball you kicked into Never Never Land, so the next time the ball goes out of bounds, she may be nowhere to be found. Remember, every second counts.

Don't put the ball in the opposing goalkeeper's hands! When you are clinging to a lead and you get the ball deep in the opponent's territory, you absolutely must make them *earn* their way out of it. The last thing in the world you want to do is let their goalkeeper get her hands on the ball, because she's the one player who can pick it up and punt it 60 yards. My advice is that you simply refuse to cross the ball. Think about it. You have the ball in the corner, six yards off the opponent's endline. If you cross it, you give the goalkeeper a chance to snatch it. Then she's going to run to the top of the 18 and hoof the ball to the far side of the center circle and now your team is under instant pressure. You're better off doing almost anything else. Take it to the corner and shield it. Poke it out for a throw-in. Heck, even giving up a goal kick is better than conceding a punt. Don't let the goalkeeper put the ball two-thirds of the way down the field with one swing of her foot.

Generally speaking, unless you have an unquestionably phenomenal opportunity to score an easy, easy goal from close range, then my advice is that you don't even put the ball into the 18. Take it to the corners and eat up clock. You don't need to win by more than one. One is plenty.

Note for Coaches: There are multiple ways to train clock management. One is in small-sided games of 5v5 to 7v7. When one team scores, it isn't allowed to score again until the opponent scores or until a specified amount of time has expired. Another way is full-sided situational games where you assign a score and the time remaining (Red Team is losing 1-0 with five minutes to play). These exercises apply to all of the Clock Management chapters.

CHAPTER 51

CLOCK MANGEMENT FOR GOALKEEPERS

Make sure your goalkeeper reads this chapter.

If there is one thing that drives me mental, it's when my goalkeeper picks up the ball and tries to milk the clock to preserve a one-goal lead. Once that ball is in your hands, make sure it's on its way back down the field in six seconds. Don't give the referee an excuse to award your opponent a free-kick from inside your 18. It's just not worth it. I'd rather leave two or three more seconds on the clock than give away that free-kick. Get your punt away and put your trust in your teammates to close out the game.

For goalkeepers, the time to kill clock is *before* you have the ball in your hands. Use your feet to control nonthreatening balls that roll into your 18. Find ways to avoid the ball-shaggers when the ball goes out for goal kicks. This is your chance to knock fifteen or more seconds off the game clock. Instead of chasing the ball when it rolls across your endline, go the opposite way. Run to the top of the 18 and shout at your defenders for some mistake they did or didn't make. For the love of Pete, don't be in a hurry to get your hands on the ball.

Watch professional soccer. You will see goalkeepers who are superb at bleeding time off the clock. Pay attention and implement their tricks into your games when appropriate.

Note for Coaches: Have this talk with your goalkeeper or someday you'll probably wish you had.

CHAPTER 52

CLOCK MANAGEMENT WHEN TRAILING

The easiest way to address this topic would be to say, "Take everything in the previous two chapters and reverse it." But I think we can do better than that.

When you're winning you try to take time off the clock. When you're losing you try to keep time on the clock. Simple enough. Aside from the obvious requirements of playing with urgency and taking restarts quickly, here are some basic strategies that too many players don't know.

Don't foul unless absolutely necessary. Only foul as a last resort. There is almost no easier way for a team to run seconds off the clock than free-kicks. Each one of them should eat up at least thirty seconds. More often than not a foul will do your team more harm than good.

Take a forgivable yellow card. If you're not already in the referee's book, this is one way to cope with desperation. When the opponent is awarded a free-kick, refuse to give up the ten yards. The referee will stop the clock and book you, but let's face it, you stopped the clock.

Be wise in your shot selection. The easiest way to run off clock is goal kicks. It happens all the time. A team desperate for the equalizer is doggedly pressuring the opponent – knocking on the door – and then the ball pops out to a center midfielder. In a complete panic she hits an off-balance shot from 30 yards that sails wide of the goal. It's an immature decision that can derail your chances of tying the game. It lets the opponent catch its breath. It lets the opponent kill clock. And it kills all the momentum your team had been building. In short, it completely lets the opponent off the hook. Even when you're desperate you must still keep your composure, make good decisions and be realistic about your abilities.

Retrieve the ball for the opponent. Make it difficult for the opponent to burn clock with their restarts. When possible and prudent, retrieve the ball for her and put it on the ground exactly where it will be restarted.

Make the goalkeeper pick up the ball. You've got to chase every ball that goes into your opponent's 18. By rule, goalkeepers have six seconds to release the ball once it is in their hands, and referees commonly grant them an extra three or four seconds. But that clock doesn't start until the goalkeeper has actually picked up the ball. The opposing goalkeeper won't use her hands until she is forced into it. To keep her from bleeding the clock, you've got to make her pick up the ball.

Set pieces must be on frame. When you are trailing late in the game and your team is awarded a free-kick in dangerous shooting range, don't get cute. Have the teammate who is best equipped to score from these situations step up and hit it. And if she doesn't score, at the very least she has to put her kick on frame. She absolutely must make the goalkeeper make a save. If the shot is on frame, at least it has a chance. It gives the goalkeeper a chance to screw it up. It might produce a rebound or a dangerous deflection. But if the shot goes over the goal, the opportunity is completely wasted and a lot of time will bleed off the clock.

Don't be afraid to sell out. When you get to the final 60 seconds of that must-win game and you're down a goal, you've got to take risks. You've got to be willing to lose by two or you won't give yourself the best chance to tie the score. If your team has a corner kick or free-kick, bring everyone including the goalkeeper into the opponent's 18. If you're going to lose, don't leave any bullets in the chamber.

Note for Coaches: Don't just wing it. Before a game even begins you should have a plan for what you'll do if you're trailing in the final few minutes. It's a good idea to occasionally dedicate a segment of training to these emergency situations so your players will have some idea of what to do.

CHAPTER 53

SCORING GOALS

All of your smart decisions and all of your hard work won't win you the game if you don't eventually put the ball into the net. Shooting requires technique, but that technique can't stand on its own. When you're in front of the goal with the ball at your feet, you've still got to make decisions that will give that ball the best chance of finding the net. Here are five simple tips to help you convert chances into goals.

Expect the Ball - Things happen very quickly when you're near the goal. Defenders are going to play with extreme urgency so you won't always have the chance to take two touches. Often, if you don't get your shot off with your first touch, you won't get the shot off at all. When you're close to the goal, the ball frequently arrives at your feet unannounced as the result of a deflection, a mis-clearance or a rebound. You've got to be mentally and physically prepared to react in a split-second. *Expect the ball to find you* and position your body to shoot with your first touch. That may mean dropping a few steps away from the goal to change your angle of support so that you can square your hips to the goal when you shoot. When you're that close to the goal, you don't want to be facing the sideline when you receive the ball. Ask yourself, "If the ball comes to me right now, can I shoot it with my first touch?" That will put you in a position to capitalize on any ball that comes your way.

Make the Goalie Make a Save – At Ole Miss we had one of the most talented and technical players I've ever coached (I'll call her Abby). Abby was a magician. She could do anything with the ball. She could screw defenders into the ground with her 1v1 dribbling. She could smack a ball with any surface of either foot. Full volleys, half-volleys, side volleys – it didn't matter. Abby was as complete a technical player as I've ever coached and that made her a joy to watch. But in front of goal the poor girl was snake-bitten. She just couldn't find a way to put the ball in the net. Now Abby wasn't the first player I've coached who suffered from this malady, but there was a difference.

Most players who can't seem to score, lack either craft or composure in front of goal – usually both. They have no idea where they should even be aiming so when the ball comes off their foot, it's a crapshoot. They shank their shots six yards wide of the goal or they bomb balls ten yards over the crossbar or they hit them directly at the goalkeeper. They use the wrong surface or choose power over placement. They lack composure and savvy. None of this was Abby's problem. Abby's problem was quite the opposite. Abby knew exactly where the ball was supposed to go and what surface she should employ to get it there. So why did this amazing player struggle in front of goal when it seems she did everything right? Well, Abby's problem was that she tried to be *too* precise. When she was close to the goal she always shot low to the corners, which is normally a very good thing. But Abby gave herself no margin for error. She constantly aimed for a microscopic shooting window in the lower corner of the goal. And often she missed that window by about four inches. Thus, Abby had more shots hit the post than any player I've ever seen. Time after time after time, in practices and games, Abby would slide the ball neatly past the goalkeeper only to see it hit the post and ricochet out of bounds.

When I started working with Abby, my first job was to convince her that she was giving goalkeepers way too much credit. She had, relatively speaking, a lot more of the goal to shoot at. Abby had to start making the goalie make a save. It didn't matter how close her shots were to being on goal if they weren't actually on goal. No ball has the chance to score unless it goes between the posts and under the crossbar. Abby needed to start leaving herself some margin for error. I told her as I'm telling you; you don't get more points if the ball touches the post on the way into the goal. All goals are worth one.

If the goalie doesn't have to make a save, you've done her job for her. When you force the goalie to make a save – in other words, when you put your shots on goal – a world of opportunity unfurls before you. Have you ever had to play goalkeeper? It's really stinking difficult! You get about a half-second to see where the ball is going, react to it, and then put enough of a body part behind the ball to keep it out of the goal. That's not an easy thing to do by any stretch of the imagination.

When you get your shots on frame, you force the goalkeeper to do a job – a very difficult one – and she might not rise to the occasion. You also give her the chance to be a normal, fallible human being. In other words, you give her a chance to screw it all up even when she should make the save. When your shot is on frame, it at least has the chance to score. Not only that – it also has the chance to take a freak bounce; it has the chance to skip through the keeper's legs; it has a chance to squirt right through her hands – all of which is better than sending it over the endline for a goal kick.

When you have the chance to score, you have got to have the composure to put the ball on goal. For most players that means sacrificing a little power for accuracy. It doesn't matter how hard you hit the ball if it sails over the bar. You don't get points for height and distance. Make the goalie make a save. Ironically it will help you score more goals. It will also produce rebound chances that will turn into goals.

Don't Shoot Hand-High – One of the great recurring frustrations of my coaching career has been watching players fail to score on excellent chances by putting their shots hand-high. Hand-high is that area on either side of the goalkeeper's body from just below hip height (where your hand is when your arm is hanging straight down) to shoulder height. Do you want to know why you shouldn't shoot there? Because that's where her hands are! Goalkeepers LOVE it when you shoot hand-high! It makes them look really, really good!

Try this little test: Stand up with your hands at your sides and see how long it takes you to bring one hand up to shoulder height (as if you were catching a baseball). Then, starting from the same position, see how long it takes you to get that same hand down to the floor. It'll take you at least twice as long to get your hand down to the floor. The same applies to goalkeepers.

If you put a shot 18 inches wide of the goalkeeper and hand-high, guess what – she's going to make a simple reflex save. But if you put that same shot on the ground, now the goalkeeper has to clear her feet out of the way and fling her body down to the ground to get her hands to the ball. That's a lot more difficult, right?

When you shoot hand-high, you make the goalie's life easy. So don't.

Shoot Against the Goalkeeper's Momentum – If you enter the 18 on the dribble at an angle that takes you across the face of the goal, cut your shot back to the far post. Let's say your dribble is angled to the west; then the goalkeeper will also be moving her body to the west. If you shoot to the west corner of the goal, the goalkeeper already has a running start and a superb chance to make the save. But if you can cut your shot back to the east corner of the goal, the goalkeeper now has to stop her feet, stop all the momentum that was heading west and then immediately leap to the east. It's one of the most difficult saves for a goalkeeper to make and one reason why so many goals are scored this way.

You can apply the same principle to crosses that make it across the face of the goal. The goalkeeper's movement is going to mirror that of the cross. Often times, if you can shoot back toward the direction of the cross, the goalkeeper will be incapable of changing direction to make the save. When you shoot back against the goalkeeper's momentum, she'll be hard-pressed to make the save.

Create an Own-Goal – If you find yourself close to the goal but at an impossible angle, like a yard off the end-line, and you absolutely must release the ball, try this: Smack the ball low and hard across the face of the goal, just in front of the goalkeeper. There will be an avalanche of bodies flooding into the six-yard box and they'll all be headed straight for the goal. The ball may find its way to one of your teammates. On the other hand, it may not have to. You may be able to create an own-goal by banging the ball off the shins of a helpless defender. Unless the ball finds its way through all that traffic and out the other side, it has an excellent chance of ending up in the goal.

Note for Coaches: Games are won and lost inside the 18s. I'm a big proponent of small-sided games such as 5v5 + GK because so much of the field is within shooting range and so many scoring chances are created. Forwards need to spend time in front of goal in game-like environments. Small-sided games are outstanding arenas to replicate the situations players will see in actual matches and they give you excellent opportunities to coach shooting decisions.

CHAPTER 54

PROTECT YOUR THINKER

"One concussion can derail an entire season."
Steve Holeman – UGA Soccer

There's one guaranteed way for you not to help your team, and that's by not being on the field. You're on a soccer team because you enjoy playing soccer. You don't get to do that unless you take care of your body – and that includes your head.

In October of 2011 I was taking our Georgia defenders through a heading exercise. I would punt the ball in the air and the defender would move to get under it and then head it back to me. I wasn't punting the ball very far or very high and each player only took five or six repetitions. It was a pretty routine drill. A few minutes later, our starting center-back complained of a headache. A few minutes after that she was diagnosed with a concussion and forced to sit out of our game the following night. I was stunned! All she had done was head five balls that were soft-punted to her. On my honor none of those punts got higher than 35 yards off the ground! I couldn't believe such a mundane drill had cost me our top defender! A year later we lost another starting defender in a similar heading exercise.

I was stunned because these drills are commonplace in soccer. Tens of thousands of players across the country were doing these exact same drills. How many of them sustained concussions? More importantly, how many of those concussions went undiagnosed?

Seven of our players were diagnosed with concussions over a four-year span. Seven! In 2014, a concussion cost us a starting center-back for three weeks! We were fortunate to have a top-flight training staff on hand at all times to diagnose these injuries and immediately begin the recovery protocol. Your team might not be so lucky.

Concussions plague more than four million Americans each year – and those are just the ones that get reported. Many remain undiagnosed. The occurrence of concussions in soccer is remarkably high. Soccer ranks only behind football in the amount of concussions sustained and it is the leading sport for concussions in females. A recent lawsuit against FIFA and US Soccer claims that in 2010, 50,000 high school soccer players suffered concussions. 50,000! And to make matters worse, once you sustain your first concussion, you are two to three times as likely to sustain subsequent concussions.

If you think that heading the ball isn't a concussion risk, Google *'concussions in soccer from heading.'* The estimated impact speed of heading a soccer ball is 70 m.p.h. You don't have to be a doctor to understand that this type of behavior isn't exactly conducive to great health. The latest research focuses on 'sub-concussive' hits. These are mini-hits to the brain, like the kind you get from heading the ball. They're not enough to ring your bell, but they do take their toll on the brain. Enough of these hits will eventually lead to a full-blown concussion. The bottom line is that soccer is a high-risk sport for brain injuries, and heading the ball is an inherent concussion risk. I know – because I've seen it happen too many times.

Concussion protocol dictates that a player may not return to practices or games until he or she has been symptom-free for at least a week. That's not seven days from the date of the concussion; it's seven days from when her symptoms disappear. Those symptoms can linger for weeks.

By now I hope you realize that soccer isn't just about the magic in your shoes; it's also about the decisions you make; it's about how you *think* the game. It only makes sense that you do something to protect your thinker.

Soccer is a collision sport. You are constantly running into other players, crashing to the ground, and challenging for headers. This is all part of your job and you won't ever be a great player if you don't have the courage to take these physical risks. That's just the life we've chosen. With the exception of a good warm-up and a reliable pair of shin guards, there hasn't been a whole lot you could do to protect yourself. But times have changed.

You're lucky. You are part of a generation of soccer players that is blessed with the technology that can minimize your concussion risk. Advances in head gear have given you the option to vastly reduce your chances of sustaining a concussion.

The runaway leader in protective headgear is a company called Unequal Technologies. Unequal is new to the soccer market, but its technology is already a mainstay in helmets for professional football, baseball and hockey players. Umpires in Major League Baseball use Unequal for their chest protectors. If this technology can comfortably absorb a baseball at 90 m.p.h., then I like it's chances against a soccer ball. A recent study of Pop Warner football players using Unequal's supplemental head padding resulted in a 75% decrease in concussions compared to the national youth football rate. All you really need to know is that most NFL, NHL and MLB teams use Unequal's technology and if it's good enough to protect those guys, it'll do just fine for soccer players.

Unequal's HALO is a lightweight headband for soccer players that is fortified with Kevlar® – yes, the same stuff used in bulletproof vests. I've got to believe that if Kevlar® can help keep our soldiers safe, it can keep us safe also.

I've talked with players using this product and their reviews were absolutely spectacular! Not only did those players say that they quickly forgot that they were even wearing headgear, they also saw no negative effect on their heading accuracy. As a matter of fact, some players actually became better headers because the HALO gave them more confidence to challenge for the ball. If a product can keep you safer and improve your heading ability, it's certainly worth considering.

Look, you need to protect yourself, and not just to stay on the field. Your long-term health is actually the bigger issue. Concussions are serious injuries. They can kill you. They can lead to memory loss, brain damage and other serious complications. My point is this: If you can reduce your risk of a concussion, why the heck wouldn't you?

If you're interested, I recommend you visit www.unequal.com. If you want to stay on the field, you have to get ahead of concussions. It's really that simple. The technology is available. Take advantage of it.

Note for Coaches: I never mandated that players had to wear headgear, but I think we all have a responsibility to let players and their parents know that they have the option to be safer and that the technology is out there. At least let them know they have a choice. Also, these days, when I run a heading drill, I use partially deflated soccer balls. Believe me, it helps.

CHAPTER 55

RECRUITING

If you are interested in the recruiting process, there is a multitude of books, articles, websites, services and seminars available. However, I feel obliged to leave you with some common sense tips that are too often overlooked. You'll have to talk to your coach or team manager about the first few.

If you want to be recruited, we have to be able to identify you. The easier you make it for us to identify you, the better your chances. So for starters, make sure we can read the number on the back of your jersey. A white number on a pink jersey is invisible to me from 25 yards and I have 20-10 vision. A white number on a yellow jersey is also invisible. As is a yellow number on a white jersey. Same goes if your white number is on a sky blue jersey. If your team wears a light jersey, make the number dark and readable. If your team wears a dark jersey, make sure the number is light (preferably white). No box shadows or any other effects. I don't care how pretty the number is; I only care that I can read it from across a soccer field.

Put your number on the front of your jersey or on the front of your shorts. That way, when you do something well and you're facing us, we can still write down your number. This may sound silly, but every coach has had those moments where he loses track of a player because he couldn't get a read on her jersey number and then lost her in the shuffle of bodies. Putting a number on the front of your uniform will help.

Many teams now warm-up in a t-shirt. Put a number on yours. If we get to the field in time to watch you warm-up, we want to be able to actually find you. This is especially important for goalkeepers because you get a lot more action in the warm-up than in the actual game. Make sure we know which goalkeeper you are. Speaking of...

Goalkeepers, make a point of being great during your warm-up. Coaches who are evaluating you will arrive early specifically to see you face a barrage of shots. We can learn more about your shot-stopping prowess in fifteen minutes of a warm-up than in 90 minutes of a match. The warm-up is your showcase. It is your chance to demonstrate your talents and your training habits. Don't "save yourself" for the game. Don't underwhelm us by being too cool to give your very best. I have walked away from plenty of goalkeepers based on a single warm-up. If I don't like your warm-up, I'm not staying for your game. The warm-up is your best chance to make a statement. Make it count.

After your match we may strategically place ourselves between your field and the parking lot so we can get a better look at you when you walk by. We may want to size you up. We may just want you to know we were there. When you change out of your game jersey or throw on a hoodie, we often lose our ability to identify you. Whatever you wear after the game, make sure it doesn't serve as a disguise.

If you send a DVD, please identify yourself in the video. Tell me what color shirt you are wearing, your jersey number, your position and any other distinguishing characteristics (a red hair bow, purple shoes, etc.) that will help me pick you out from the 21 other tiny strangers I see on the screen. If you do this directly on the DVD, it means I'll always know how to find you even if I lost your letter, which is a distinct possibility.

When you call me and get my voicemail, make sure you mention what grade you are in because the NCAA has strict regulations about returning phone calls. Same goes for emails. I need to know your graduation year. Put your graduation year, club team, jersey number and email address on everything you send me, including your player bio/resume.

We understand that you are going to compose a form letter/email that you will send out to a multitude of coaches. That's fine. But take the time to personalize it a wee bit. Don't write:

Dear Coach-
I am very interested in the academic opportunities and soccer program at your university.

Instead write:

Dear Coach Blank-
I am very interested in the academic opportunities and soccer program at the University of Georgia.

You get bonus points for closing your note with something like *Go Bulldogs!* (or Buckeyes or Bruins or whatever).

Your primary goal for the initial phase of recruiting is to get coaches to watch you play. In the weeks leading up to the major showcase tournaments we get 200+ emails from prospects asking us to watch them play. There's obviously no way we can see all of them so we've got to prioritize. If there are two otherwise equal prospects, the one who we have a better chance of signing becomes the priority. Anything in your email that shows you have a genuine interest in my university helps move your letter toward the top of the pile. Here are examples from emails that got my attention:

- *Congratulations on your great year in the SEC and your win over So And So University!*

- *I was at your match against So And So University and was very impressed at how well your team possessed the ball.*

- *I watched the Bulldogs play on television three times this fall…*

- *Georgia's excellent Pre-Veterinary program is a perfect fit for my academic goals.*

And finally, for the love of Pete, remember to change those personalized touches from one university to the next! Make sure your email is addressed to the appropriate coach at the appropriate university. At least twice a year I get an email from a prospect telling me how the University of Alabama/Virginia/Colorado/North Carolina would be a good fit for her. Great. I'll be sure to let them know.

Always sign your emails with your name, your graduation year, the name of your club and your jersey number. It helps college coaches to commit you to memory. Here's an example:

Sincerely,

Dan Blank - 2014
#7, Hamilton F.C.

When you hit send on your email, make sure we don't see that your email is going to 50 other coaches. Take the extra five minutes to send it to one coach at a time. If you personalize the email, this will come naturally. If I see your email has gone to even one more university, I'm hitting delete. I'm funny that way.

Your email address represents you. Make sure it speaks well of you. Addresses like partygurl@aol.com and boycrazy@gmail.com will not endear you to prospective coaches.

Your two primary objectives in the initial stages of recruiting should be to get seen by the right coaches and to not disqualify yourself along the way. Pay attention to the details.

One last piece of advice… College soccer will be one of the very best experiences of your life. Attack it with enthusiasm and passion. Give your best to it every day and you'll never regret it.

A FINAL WORD

This may be the skinniest soccer book ever written so I genuinely hope you feel you've gotten your money's worth. I hope you found something in these pages that will make you a smarter player or coach. Soccer is full of moments that call out for nuanced decisions. Your brain is every bit as important as your feet. You should strive to maximize your abilities as a thinking player. If you enjoyed *Soccer iQ* and found value in it, I hope you will take a moment to leave a 5-star review on Amazon, because that's like throwing a fiver in my tip jar. Now that you've finished reading, I invite you to take the free *Soccer iQ* quiz at www.soccerpoet.com.

To the coaches – I am acutely aware that some concepts (in addition to grammar and punctuation) were overlooked in the authorship of this book and that you wouldn't be a coach if you didn't look forward to pointing out these oversights. I am also aware that plenty of you will disagree with some of the ideas I have presented. Fantastic! I invite you to visit www.soccerpoet.com and express your thoughts. Many coaches have ordered copies of *Soccer iQ* for their entire team. If you'd like to place a bulk order of 20 or more copies for your team at a discounted price, just send me an email at coach@soccerpoet.com.

A special thank you goes out to Steve Holeman, Steve Nugent and Robin Confer who were instrumental in identifying topics for this text. *"That should be a chapter!"* became the signature shout of our *Aha!* moments as we watched dozens of games and training sessions while this book took shape. Brenda Gurr has been a treasured friend, assistant and editor in almost all of my writing projects including this one and has my eternal gratitude. A special word of thanks to Aaron Usiskin, an extremely talented graphic designer who, in the 11th hour, saved the day! I'm pretty sure Aaron is also the fittest graphic designer in the free world. Aaron is not to be blamed for the diagrams in this text. Those cave art renderings are entirely mine. And thank you to Graham Ramsay for teaching me so much about the game I thought I knew.

Finally I would like to thank my wife, Beth, for going to bed alone for a few weeks while her brand new husband stayed up late to write this book.

If you've got questions or comments, please email me at coach@soccer-poet.com. Also, I hope you'll be my Twitter friend. My handle is @SoccerPoet.

Other Books by Dan Blank
Available at www.soccerpoet.com

Soccer iQ Volume II — Since Soccer iQ debuted, many coaches have provided suggestions for an awesome second volume, and this is it.

Everything Your Coach Never Told You Because You're a Girl — This is what your coach would have said to you if you were a boy, told through the story of a small-college soccer team that won more games than it ever had a right to win.

Happy Feet — How to be a Gold Star Soccer Parent (Everything the Coach, the Ref and Your Kid Want You to Know) — The book every soccer parent needs to read.

Rookie — Surviving Your Freshman Year of College Soccer — If you're planning to play college soccer, do yourself a favor and read this. I'm trying to help you. By the way, this makes a great Signing Day gift.

In My Tribe — Developing a Culture of Kickass in Female Athletes — The follow-up to Everything You're Coach Never Told You Because You're a Girl, this book details the specific tools employed to feed our competitive beast. Available 2015.

Possession — Teaching Your Team to Keep the Darn Ball — A step by step explanation of coaching points and on-field exercises for possession soccer.

Shutout Pizza — Soccer Defending for Teams that Hate Conceding Goals — Ole Miss led the SEC in goals-against average in 2009. Georgia did it in 2010. This is the book those players used to become the league's best defense. Available in 2015.

ABOUT THE AUTHOR

Dan Blank has been coaching college soccer for over twenty years. He is the only coach in Southeastern Conference history to lead the conference's best defense in consecutive years at different universities (Ole Miss 2009, Georgia 2010). He has an 'A' License from the USSF and an Advanced National Diploma from the NSCAA. You can buy his books and read his blog at www.soccerpoet.com.

Made in the USA
Middletown, DE
14 June 2015